W9-AGT-056

DISCARD

Shel Silverstein

WHO
WROTE
THAT?

WHO WROTE THAT?

Shel Silverstein

Elisa Ludwig

Foreword by
Kyle Zimmer

Chelsea House Publishers
Philadelphia

CHELSEA HOUSE PUBLISHERS

VP, NEW PRODUCT DEVELOPMENT Sally Cheney
DIRECTOR OF PRODUCTION Kim Shinners
CREATIVE MANAGER Takeshi Takahashi
MANUFACTURING MANAGER Diann Grasse

STAFF FOR SHEL SILVERSTEIN

EDITOR Benjamin Kim
PICTURE RESEARCHER Pat Holl
PRODUCTION EDITOR Megan Emery
SERIES DESIGNER Keith Trego
LAYOUT 21st Century Publishing and Communications, Inc.

http://www.chelseahouse.com

First Printing

1 3 5 7 9 8 6 4 2

Library of Congress Cataloging-in-Publication Data

Ludwig, Elisa.
  Shel Silverstein / by Elisa Ludwig.
     p. cm. — (Who wrote that?)
Includes index.
Contents: Dragged kicking and screaming — A Boy named Shel — The rise
of Uncle Shelby — Branching out — The sidewalk and the houseboat —
Out of the attic — Things change — To rhyme one more time.
  ISBN 0-7910-7624-5
 1. Silverstein, Shel—Juvenile literature. 2. Authors, American—20th cen-
tury—Biography—Juvenile literature. 3. Children's stories—Authorship—
Juvenile literature. [1. Silverstein, Shel. 2. Authors,
American.] I. Title. II. Series.
  PS3569.I47224Z76 2003
  818'.5409—dc22   2003019351

Table of Contents

FOREWORD BY
KYLE ZIMMER
PRESIDENT, FIRST BOOK

HUMANITY IS POWERED by stories. From our earliest days as thinking beings, we employed every available tool to tell each other stories. We danced, drew pictures on the walls of our caves, spoke, and sang. All of this extraordinary effort was designed to entertain, recount the news of the day, explain natural occurrences—and then gradually to build religious and cultural traditions and establish the common bonds and continuity that eventually formed civilizations. Stories are the most powerful force in the universe; they are the primary element that has distinguished our evolutionary path.

Our love of the story has not diminished with time. Enormous segments of societies are devoted to the art of storytelling. Book sales in the United States alone topped $26 billion last year; movie studios spend fortunes to create and promote stories; and the news industry is more pervasive in its presence than ever before.

There is no mystery to our fascination. Great stories are magic. They can introduce us to new cultures, or remind us of the nobility and failures of our own, inspire us to greatness or scare us to death, but above all, stories provide human insight on a level that is unavailable through any other source. In fact, stories connect each of us to the rest of humanity not just in our own time, but also throughout history.

This special magic of books is the greatest treasure that we can hand down from generation to generation. In fact, that spark in a child that comes from books became the motivation for the creation of my organization, First Book, a national literacy program with a simple mission: to provide new books to the most disadvantaged children. At present, First Book has been at work in hundreds of communities for over a decade. Every year children in need receive millions of books through our organization and millions more are provided through dedicated literacy institutions across the United States and around the world. In addition, groups of people dedicate themselves tirelessly to working with children to share reading and stories in every imaginable setting from schools to the streets. Of course, this Herculean effort serves many important goals. Literacy translates to productivity and employability in life and many other valid and even essential elements. But at the heart of this movement are people who love stories, love to read, and want desperately to ensure that no one misses the wonderful possibilities that reading provides.

When thinking about the importance of books, there is an overwhelming urge to cite the literary devotion of great minds. Some have written of the magnitude of the importance of literature. Amy Lowell, an American poet, captured the concept with her statement when she said, "Books are more than books. They are the life, the very heart and core of ages past, the reason why men lived and worked and died, the essence and quintessence of their lives." Others have spoken of their personal obsession with books, as in Thomas Jefferson's simple statement: "I live for books." But more compelling, perhaps, is the almost instinctive excitement in children for books and stories.

Throughout my years at First Book, I have heard truly extraordinary stories about the power of books in the lives of children. In one case, a homeless child, who had been bounced from one location to another, later resurfaced—and the only possession that he had fought to keep was the book he was given as part of a First Book distribution months earlier. More recently, I met a child who, upon receiving the book he wanted, flashed a big smile and said, "This is my big chance!" These snapshots reveal the true power of books and stories to give hope and change lives.

As these children grow up and continue to develop their love of reading, they will owe a profound debt to those volunteers who reached out to them—a debt that they may repay by reaching out to spark the next generation of readers. But there is a greater debt owed by all of us— a debt to the storytellers, the authors, who have bound us together, inspired our leaders, fueled our civilizations, and helped us put our children to sleep with their heads full of images and ideas.

WHO WROTE THAT? is a series of books dedicated to introducing us to a few of these incredible individuals. While we have almost always honored stories, we have not uniformly honored storytellers. In fact, some of the most important authors have toiled in complete obscurity throughout their lives or have been openly persecuted for the uncomfortable truths that they have laid before us. When confronted with the magnitude of their written work or perhaps the daily grind of our own, we can forget that writers are people. They struggle through the same daily indignities and dental appointments, and they experience the intense joy and bottomless despair that many of us do. Yet somehow they rise above it all to deliver a powerful thread that connects us all. It is a rare honor to have the opportunity that these books provide to share the lives of these extraordinary people. Enjoy.

Shel Silverstein's friend, children's author and fellow cartoonist Tomi Ungerer, poses with one of his works at Strasbourg's Modern and Contemporary Art Museum. In 1963, Ungerer convinced Silverstein to meet with his editor, Ursula Nordstrom of Harper & Row. The meeting marked the start of Silverstein's career as a children's author/illustrator.

Dragged Kicking and Screaming

Some things you can say through drawings, and some things you need the extensiveness of writing. I don't know if I'm saying different things in the way that is most fitting. I say things through poetry, I say them through song, I say them through drawing. [1]
— *Shel Silverstein*

SHEL SILVERSTEIN HAD no idea what he was getting himself into. His friend Tomi Ungerer kept insisting that Shel meet his editor and she would show him what a great idea it was. Tomi was a French cartoonist and a children's book author whose books had become famous internationally. He wanted

Shel Silverstein, who was already a cartoonist, to become a children's book author, too. As they rode the elevator up to the editor's office, Shel Silverstein wondered if Tomi was right. The last thing Silverstein had ever wanted to do was write children's books. But Tomi was adamant, so Shel was humoring him. He would meet with the editor in New York City and satisfy Tomi, and then he would go back to Chicago and forget about it, and keep drawing his cartoons.

Silverstein was thirty-one years old, a tall, tanned, and athletic looking man. His shiny, bald head was complemented by a bushy, dark beard, and he had thick eyebrows to match. He wore baggy clothes and had the look of someone who was both relaxed and artistic.

It was 1963, and Shel Silverstein had the reputation of a bohemian, a man who was more creative than conventional. It would be a few years before hippies were in fashion, and Americans began protesting the Vietnam War, but Silverstein was a hippie before his time. He believed in racial desegregation and civil rights. He hung out in coffeehouses and played folk songs and laughed at what he considered the "square" conventions of most people. He didn't believe in getting married, settling down, and moving to the suburbs, and his views were unusual for the day.

Unlike other beatniks of the time, however, Silverstein believed in working hard to attain his goals, in honing his skills. He was not interested in just sitting around. Through his work, he wanted to express himself and he believed in total freedom of expression. He believed in his own freedom; in his ability to travel and enjoy the world. He was friends with many artists, disc jockeys, musicians, and journalists, and he was well-liked. He liked to tell jokes and surprise people, and his easy nature attracted new people all the time—so much so that he had friends in every city.

Shel Silverstein followed his own sense of individuality. Well into the 1990s, long after being a hippie was no longer in style, and long after Silverstein had become a famous and wealthy writer, he wore the same baggy clothes. The clothes, which seemed so out of place for a successful writer, were his trademark.

Silverstein's friend, songwriter Fred Koller once said, "If you saw Shel coming up a New York sidewalk with his old mailman's bag stuffed full of songs, wearing a worn-out pair of cowboy boots and faded Can't-Bust-'Em jeans, you'd never guess that he'd written dozens of hit records and sold over eighteen million children's books."

On this day in the early 1960s, it would be difficult for Shel Silverstein himself to guess that he would sell so many children's books that he eventually would be able to afford designer clothes—mostly because he had no interest in writing them. But Shel and Tomi were at the editor's office now, and it was time for their meeting.

The editor, whose name was Ursula Nordstrom, greeted the pair and looked over Silverstein's cartoons. Nordstrom was a famous children's book editor at Harper & Row publishing house who would, over the course of her career, edit *Where the Wild Things Are* and *Harriet the Spy*, as well as books by E.B. White, Laura Ingalls Wilder, and Louise Fitzhugh. Nordstrom believed it was important to publish comical, entertaining children's books that showed children being bad as well as good, and tell stories that had more to offer than just a moral. Her work, introducing new and exciting authors to readers, would change children's literature forever.

After looking over Silverstein's art, Ursula Nordstrom agreed with Tomi Ungerer: She was sure that Shel Silverstein would make a terrific children's author and illustrator. Nordstrom had in fact admired Silverstein's work for at least four years, but it had taken her that long to arrange the meeting through Ungerer. Silverstein was still not quite convinced, but he thought he would give it a try. At least he would be able to get some of his work published. And it was better, he thought, to have his art out there as a way to communicate his ideas to others than not at all. In the end, he agreed to write children's books.

He went back to Chicago and got to work. It never took him long to come up with a new idea, and soon he had written and illustrated a book, which he sent back to Ursula Nordstrom. Later that same year, Silverstein's first children's book, *Lafcadio, the Lion Who Shot Back*, was published.

Silverstein would have had no way of knowing that this meeting in Ursula Nordstrom's office was just the beginning of the most celebrated part of his career. After all, it would have been difficult to imagine being successful at something he had never even thought about doing. And he had already established himself as a cartoonist and musician—these were the careers he expected to be remembered for. In a rare interview he gave in 1975, Silverstein would relate the story to Jean F. Mercier, a writer from *Publishers Weekly*. "I never planned to write or draw for kids. Tomi Ungerer practically dragged me, kicking and screaming into Ursula Nordstrom's office."

Did you know...

Shel Silverstein wrote hundreds of songs that have been recorded by more than ninety different artists.

Even with Ursula Nordstrom's encouragement, writing for children would take some getting used to. At the time of his meeting at Nordstrom's office, Shel Silverstein had already written two books and illustrated a third, though they were intended for adults. He was also working as a cartoonist for *Playboy* magazine. The free-spirited Silverstein would travel around the world and draw humorous cartoons about his attempts to understand foreign culture and meet foreign women. Though they were a favorite of readers of the magazine, the cartoons were not appropriate for children's books.

Silverstein had written another book called *Uncle Shelby's ABZ Book: A Primer for Tender Young Minds*. The book was also originally published in *Playboy* magazine. It looked like an illustrated children's book, modeled after the old-fashioned alphabet primers, where each page was devoted to a letter of the alphabet, and illustrated with words and pictures. This primer, however, was actually a satire of children's books and was not intended for children. Silverstein advised his readers in E for Eggs to throw eggs at the ceiling, in F for Fingers to pick their noses, and in K for Kidnappers to tell the strange men in cars passing by that their fathers were rich. In what was to become Silverstein's signature style, it both comically broke and made fun of the rules. Children eventually did get hold of the book, and even though adults feared they would not understand the jokes, they understood that Silverstein was not truly advising them to get in the car with a kidnapper.

Nordstrom saw the humor in Silverstein's work, and she seemed to understand how to uncover the children's author inside the adult satirist. Soon after, Silverstein submitted a draft of *Lefcadio, the Lion Who Shot Back*. In their correspondences between drafts, Nordstrom would suggest changes to Silverstein, particularly when his story seemed too adult-focused for the audience he was writing for. Silverstein would go back and rewrite, and return with another draft of his work. This was a pattern they would repeat with each of his children's books, and together, the pair worked efficiently and developed a mutual admiration for one another.

As a cartoonist, Shel Silverstein's early cartoons displayed his wry and often cynical way of looking at the world, usually in stark black and white drawings. The simple, sometimes silly line drawings of his cartooning days would also show up in the illustrations for his children's books. His writing and his drawing were well-suited to one another, and in his children's books his two talents came together as two halves of a whole. Often the drawing works as a punch line for the words that follow, with an unexpected twist popping up.

Ungerer and Nordstrom were right. It was not long before Silverstein was channeling his creativity in a whole new way. Once he'd accepted the fact that he was doing it, the transition to writing for children felt pretty natural. To everyone else it seemed almost preordained.

With Nordstrom's help, Silverstein managed to carry over what was best about his adult work into his children's books. What remained the same was his offbeat sense of humor and unexpected twists. He didn't spare his young readers the odd and not always happy endings of his adult cartoons. Over the years, readers would comment that this was precisely what made Silverstein's works so appealing: He treated his young readers as if they were adults and in on the joke. This was an unusual feature for children's literature at the time, which held as its central tenet the idea that children were fragile, impressionable, and unable to distinguish between books and reality. Silverstein, of course, felt quite the opposite, and if children were at all fragile or impressionable it was because adults had protected them from reality. In the end, it was perhaps Shel Silverstein's very reluctance to write children's books that made his children's books so different.

Today, Shel Silverstein is best known for the work that Ursula Nordstrom and Tomi Ungerer dragged, kicking and screaming out of him. For more than thirty years, young readers have enjoyed the poetry collections *Where the Sidewalk Ends* and *A Light in the Attic*, as well as the best-selling illustrated fable *The Giving Tree*.

But Shel Silverstein's work took many different forms, and children's books, his claim to fame, were only a small portion of his creative output. Because of his multiple talents, some admirers have called him a genius. Many others have called him a Renaissance man. Like Leonardo Da Vinci, he was able to do several different things and do them well. It was as if Shel Silverstein was constantly bubbling over with ideas and images, and only needed a way to express them—it almost didn't matter how.

For instance, Shel Silverstein was a highly accomplished musician. He played several different instruments, including guitar, piano, trombone, and saxophone. He recorded fourteen albums of his music and supplied songs for other musicians to record. The multitalented musician's songwriting skills were applied to Hollywood, where he scored a number of major motion pictures, including: *Ned Kelly* (1970), *Who Is Harry Kellerman and Why Is He Saying Such Terrible Things About Me?* (1971), *Thieves* (1977), and *Postcards From the Edge* (1990). Silverstein even had a brief turn as an actor, appearing in *Who Is Harry Kellerman and Why Is He Saying Such Terrible Things About Me?* alongside Dustin Hoffman and as a regular on a radio program called *The Jean Shepherd Show*.

Starting in the 1980s, Silverstein went on to write nearly two dozen plays. During this period, he collaborated on his own screenplay called *Things Change* with the famous playwright and scriptwriter David Mamet, best known for

Silverstein's talents weren't limited to writing and illustrating. A true "Renaissance man," he was a skilled musician, capable on several instruments, including guitar, which he plays here with film star Dustin Hoffman on the set of Who Is Harry Kellerman and Why Is He Saying Such Terrible Things About Me?

writing the films *The Untouchables*, *Glengarry Glen Ross*, and *Wag the Dog*.

Beginning in 1963, until his death in 1999, however, Shel Silverstein continued to write children's books. In all, Silverstein wrote eleven works for children. Many of these were recorded as albums of songs and poems.

To Silverstein, his talents were connected. "I do believe that a person who is truly observant in one of the arts will be truly observant and sensitive in the others as well, but it's his ability to express these things that would limit him. I believe that a man who is a sensitive painter is sensitive to life, and therefore would be sensitive as a writer or as a storyteller." [2]

Silverstein was able to express himself in many different ways. Whether it was a book or a song he wrote, each remains uniquely Shel Silverstein's. The bohemian artist always insisted on doing things his own way. When he became well-known, Silverstein began to refuse giving interviews and making appearances on television shows. Instead, he decided that his work, in all its many forms, would speak for itself. Today, it still does.

Comiskey Park, home of the Chicago White Sox from 1910 to 1990, was like a second home for the young Silverstein. A devoted fan, he attended as many games as he could and had dreams of playing for the White Sox when he grew up. Later, he would end up working at the stadium as a hot-dog vendor.

2

A Boy Named Shel

[The Army] did me good, taught me things about life and gave me the freedom to create. [3]

—*Shel Silverstein*

SHEL SILVERSTEIN FELT seasick, partly from the giant waves beneath the boat and partly from anxiety. He was twenty-three years old, and on his first military mission. The ship was bound for Yokohama, Japan. The soldiers on board were being sent off to fight the Korean War. Shel Silverstein had trained at two different army bases in the United States, but still, there was no way of knowing what might lie ahead, and this was the farthest he'd ever traveled, all the way across the Pacific Ocean. As he battled nausea and tried to keep himself steady, a fellow soldier approached him. The young man introduced himself as Robert Sweeney, and after a few minutes of chatting, he revealed that he, too, felt a little uneasy about the voyage.

The two men discovered that they were both writers and they were both assigned to contribute to the ship's newspaper, so they sat down and began to write some of their impressions of the boat and their crewmates. Soon, Silverstein had produced some cartoons that he showed to Sweeney. Sweeney immediately knew that Silverstein was talented, and he passed them around the ship. It wasn't long before the rest of the ship's weary and frightened soldiers were laughing.

Shel Silverstein was born on September 25, 1930 in Logan Square, a largely immigrant neighborhood in Chicago. His parents, Nathan and Helen, were Jewish, and like many of the people in his neighborhood, were working class. Shel also had a sister named Peggy.

Not much is known about Shel Silverstein's childhood because he rarely gave interviews and seemed determined to keep his family life private. What is known is that Shel Silverstein was an imaginative child. Like most kids, he hated to do any household chores, especially taking out the garbage, a sentiment that would be captured in his famous poem, "Sarah Cynthia Sylvia Stout Would Not Take the Garbage Out." He preferred to sit and draw pictures.

In a strange way, it was most likely baseball and not an aversion to taking the garbage out that taught Shel Silverstein to be a good cartoonist. From an early age, Silverstein loved the sport. He was a devoted White Sox fan and visited the ballpark whenever he could to root for his hometown team. He wanted to be a baseball player himself and dreamed of someday joining the White Sox. By the time he was around twelve years old, though, he realized he was not a good enough athlete to ever play sports professionally, and so he reluctantly gave up his dream. He would have to settle for being an enthusiastic fan.

If he had continued playing baseball it might have improved his social life. As a teenager, Shel Silverstein was interested in girls, but since he didn't excel at sports, the girls he knew wouldn't pay much attention to him. Another sure way to attract girls in those days was to dance well, but he claimed in interviews that he couldn't do that either. Instead, he focused on the things he was good at and hoped the girls would take notice. When he wasn't going to baseball games, he continued to spend most of his time drawing pictures. He didn't have any role models or teachers in school, and he didn't know much about other cartoonists. He taught himself how to draw, and later he would be grateful that not having models to copy forced him to develop his own style. It wasn't until he was much older that Silverstein saw and learned about the work of cartoonists popular during that era, such as James Thurber and Robert Benchley. By then, he was already earning money by making his own drawings for *Playboy* and other magazines.

Shel attended Roosevelt High School, and though he was recognized as a good artist he remained unpopular with the girls. He was smart, but he was not a terribly good student. It may have been that he was so creative that he had a hard time thinking the way his teachers expected him to. After high school he went to the University of Illinois at Navy Pier to study art, but he was thrown out after one year for his poor grades. The next semester he transferred to the Chicago Academy of Fine Arts to study drawing, but he lasted at that school only another year.

Finally, he landed at Roosevelt University where he studied English for three years. At Roosevelt, Shel Silverstein was still not a great student but he found people who saw the talent in him despite his poor grades. One of his most ardent supporters was Robert Coseby, an English professor who liked Shel's work and encouraged him to continue writing. Years later, Silverstein would credit Coseby for giving him the first real push to develop his talent further. During his years at Roosevelt, Silverstein also began contributing to a monthly student paper called the *Torch*, writing stories and drawing cartoons.

Shel's first cartoon for the *Torch*, published in 1950 when he was twenty years old, shows a naked man holding a cigarette in a classroom while an angry looking professor looms nearby. The text reads "What do you mean 'No Smoking?' I thought this was a LIBERAL school." Shel was apparently poking fun at the university's policies, that a professor would be more concerned with the student smoking than with his attending class in the nude.

At the end of 1951, the *Torch* published what it considered to be the best student cartoons of the year, and two of them were Silverstein's. In 1951, Shel had also begun writing for the paper, with a column called "The Garbage Man." During the years that he was at college, America was involved in the Cold War with the Soviet Union, and Senator Joseph McCarthy had initiated his famous McCarthy hearings, accusing many public figures of being communists. Much of Shel's work slyly commented on what came to be known as the Red Scare. One satirical item in his column read,

Silverstein enrolled at Roosevelt University after failing to complete art school at two different institutions. Robert Coseby, shown here, was an English professor at Roosevelt who recognized Silverstein's writing talent and encouraged him to pursue it further.

"In answer to certain charges: next Christmas the Santa in front of the college will be dressed entirely in blue." Silverstein also made fun of the ROTC and the army, most likely knowing that he and most of his friends would eventually be drafted.

What do you mean "No Smoking!" I thought this was a LIBERAL school.

In his first cartoon for his college paper, the Roosevelt Torch, *Silverstein takes a jab at the university's policies by illustrating that the professor is more concerned with his student smoking than he is with him showing up for class naked.*

The paper was supposed to pay its contributors but the management ran out of money. Instead, they paid Shel Silverstein by giving him an old but still-working typewriter, which was very useful to a poor college student. During this time, he was also able to take some night classes across the street at the Art Institute of Chicago, furthering his drawing education.

Despite these early opportunities to learn, Silverstein regretted ever going to college and wished he had spent that time traveling the world instead. "Imagine: Four years you could have spent traveling around Europe meeting people, or going to the Far East or Africa or India, meeting people, exchanging ideas, reading all you wanted to anyway, and instead I wasted it at Roosevelt," he told an interviewer from *Aardvark* magazine.

But Shel Silverstein would get his chance to travel. In 1953, before he could finish his college degree, he was drafted into the army. As a soldier, he worked at Fort Riley in Kansas and Fort Belvoir in Virginia before being sent to Japan, and later, Korea. While in the Army, he began to work as a cartoonist and reporter for the Pacific edition of *Stars and Stripes*, a military publication that recently has been revived. He considered this job a huge responsibility, and it was his first real opportunity to work as a cartoonist.

In Tokyo, Japan, Silverstein had an *uchi*, or small room, a few blocks away from the *Stars and Stripes* printing plant. Every night he would sit in his room and develop ideas for his cartoons. He would think of one idea and then come up with twenty or thirty different jokes. He would then narrow these down into just a few cartoons, giving his characters strange and funny faces. He would share his sketches with Robert Sweeney who would help him decide which ones to turn in to the editor at the paper.

Shel Silverstein liked to stir up trouble in a good-natured way, and he used his cartoons to joke about the army. His early cartoons poked fun at officers, but he was quickly criticized for mocking his superiors, so then he decided to focus on sergeants, who were lower on the totem pole. These, too, created an angry response from his readers. "Finally I was told all I could attack were civilians and animals. But they even made zebras off limits to me because they had stripes," he told a reporter from *Stars and Stripes* some forty years later.

One cartoon that almost made him lose his job at the *Stars and Stripes* showed the wives and children of military officers wearing uniforms that had been refitted into civilian clothes. The officers who saw the cartoon were angry because they thought Silverstein was implying that officers stole uniforms and took them home to dress their families. When they threatened to court-martial Silverstein, he explained that what he really meant by the cartoon was that the officers were so enthusiastically devoted to the military that they chose to dress their families in uniforms. Considering Silverstein's playful and rebellious attitude, the officers were most likely right about the cartoon's meaning, but they took his word, and Silverstein was not court-martialed.

Shel Silverstein was not a model soldier, and he often got into trouble with his superior officers while serving in the army. One time a military police officer stopped him and asked him to lift his cuffs, and Silverstein revealed that he was wearing argyle socks with his uniform. He was reprimanded for breaking the rules. He called himself the "worst soldier in the regiment." Still, he would remember his days as a soldier fondly, especially because they gave him the chance to grow as an artist.

While he was in the army, he wrote his first book, a collection of cartoons, called *Take Ten*. The cartoons had all appeared in *Stars and Stripes* but had never been compiled in one place. His army buddy and fellow *Stars and Stripes* contributor Robert Sweeney wrote the foreword for the book. It was published in 1955 and printed at the same plant that distributed the newspaper. A year later, it was released in a paperback version called *Grab Your Socks!* By then, the Korean War had long been over, Shel Silverstein had been discharged from the army and he was living in the United States.

When he came back to Chicago in 1955, Shel Silverstein had a difficult time finding work as a cartoonist. He got a job at Comiskey Park, selling hot dogs and beer on Thursday nights. Even though his cartooning career was progressing slowly, his vending career was taking off. He was a star vendor and sold a record amount of hot dogs.

Slowly, Silverstein began to get work as a freelance cartoonist. After a year of working freelance, he met a young man named Hugh Hefner. Hefner was in the process of starting a new magazine called *Playboy*. At that time *Playboy* was a gentleman's magazine notorious for showing pictures of scantily clad women, but Hefner was also trying to create a publication that had funny, smart articles that were written by talented young journalists. The magazine and its staff were thought to be on the cutting edge of culture. When he met Shel Silverstein, Hefner recognized his talent, and soon made him a staff cartoonist and gave him an office in the Playboy Mansion, which at that time was in Chicago.

Silverstein's first cartoon in *Playboy* appeared in a booklet stapled into the August 1956 issue. He then began a travel series where he reported from countries all over the world including Japan, Switzerland, France, Russia, and Italy. The travel series continued for several years, and Silverstein

Did you know...

Some of Shel Silverstein's cartoons in the mid-1950s appeared in *Look*, *Sports Illustrated*, and *This Week* magazines.

developed a loyal audience that followed him as he went to a bullfight in Spain and a safari in Africa.

While he was in Africa in 1959, Shel got in a serious car accident. The impact shattered his leg and he was almost killed. For a few years afterward, as he recovered from his injury, he stopped traveling and contributing his travel stories to *Playboy*, instead focusing on his other cartoons and features. He also began writing music and practicing playing his new songs.

In 1959, Silverstein recorded his first album called *Hairy Jazz*. The album was mainly folk music. Two of the songs were originals that Silverstein wrote, and the others were his interpretations of other musician's songs. The album was called *Hairy Jazz* because most of the compositions he interpreted were jazz standards that he turned into folk ballads. It was an unusual album for its day, and even though it didn't sell very well, it marked Silverstein as a multitalented artist.

The work at *Playboy* continued to be challenging and interesting for Silverstein. In 1961, he started a new feature in the magazine called *Teevie Jeebies*. These were photographs taken from actual movies that were played often in those years on late-night television. Silverstein would write his own captions for each photograph, changing the meaning into his own hilarious and absurd story. These not-quite cartoons became a popular part of the magazine and were later compiled into two books.

In 1962, Silverstein got his dream assignment: The magazine was sending him to Sarasota, Florida to report on the White Sox's spring training. The cartoons he drew from that assignment show him playing on the field with the White Sox and interviewing team members with comical results. The last cartoon shows the manager telling

Silverstein, "Now the secret of good conditioning is running . . . I want you to do twenty laps on the infield . . . and keep running all the way back to Chicago, so we can get some work done here!"

He may have learned once and for all that he was not White Sox material, but Shel Silverstein was well on his way to many other successes.

Silverstein counted Ramblin' Jack Elliott, one of Bob Dylan's major influences, among his friends during his years in Greenwich Village in the early 1960s. For Silverstein, who performed in local clubs and sold songs to fellow musicians, folk music was the perfect vehicle for his antiestablishment views, which included free speech and desegregation.

3

The Rise of
Uncle Shelby

If you're behind the times, they won't notice you. If you're right in tune with them, you're no better than they are, so they won't care much for you. Be just a little ahead of them. If you're way ahead of them, you might as well be twenty miles behind them, because they don't understand what you're talking about. [4]

—*Shel Silverstein*

SHEL SILVERSTEIN WAS himself a little ahead of his time. In the early 1960s, he was living in New York City's Greenwich Village, sharing an apartment with a fellow musician named Bob Gibson. He was contributing to *Playboy* magazine on a

33

regular basis and living the life of a beatnik. After recovering from the injuries he suffered in the auto accident, he resumed traveling the world and spoke openly about the need for desegregation in America.

America was in the midst of the civil rights movement, sparked by the Montgomery Bus Boycott in 1955. African Americans were demanding their rights and protests had begun to spring up all around the country, in schools and in communities. At the same time, more people were beginning to participate in a "counterculture," questioning society and trying to live more freely than their parents had.

Even though he was associated with beatniks, Shel Silverstein had little patience for people who sat around in coffeehouses and talked about their creative and political ideas all day. He explained his frustration to an interviewer in 1963. "Thinking is not enough. Sensitivity is not enough. People want to be accepted for sensitivity, for tender thoughts, for high ideals. That's not enough. What can you do with it besides just feel it? You've got to do something with it or you'll have the greatest unpublished novel ever, and the greatest unpainted canvas. What good is that?" [5]

More than just talking about ideas, Shel Silverstein was interested in actively participating in New York's counterculture, in making and sharing art in productive ways. One of the most obvious ways, in that era, to express your political and artistic ideas was through folk music. The songs, which told stories that illustrated ideas of change and the need for revolution, were an easy way to communicate to a large audience. American folk singers had been writing songs for generations, but in the 1960s it became a fashionable art form, popularized by the success of Bob Dylan and Joan Baez, who also lived in Greenwich Village.

Shel Silverstein was attracted to folk music and quickly became deeply involved in the folk scene. Around the time Bob Dylan and Joan Baez were recording their early albums, Shel Silverstein was playing concerts regularly at famous folk music clubs like The Bitter End in New York and The Gate of Horn in Chicago. He was friends with well-known folk musicians such as Ramblin' Jack Elliott, who is widely regarded as one of Dylan's greatest influences.

Silverstein may not have had a knack for singing, and people have described his voice as gravelly or raspy. He freely admitted that he didn't have a great voice, but he enjoyed writing songs and singing them. Despite his hoarse vocals, his clever songs attracted a following. In 1962, he released an album called *Inside Folk Songs*. These were folk songs, but in true Silverstein manner, they also made fun of the folk music boom in the United States during that time. The album contained the song "Boa Constrictor" which he would include as a poem in his book, *Where the Sidewalk Ends*, more than ten years later. The album also featured "The Unicorn," a song that told the story of unicorns that were left behind when Noah built his ark:

A long time ago, when the Earth was green,
And there was more kinds of animals than you've ever seen.
And they'd run around free while the world was being born,
And the loveliest of all was the Unicorn.

There was green alligators and long-necked geese,
Hump back camels and some chimpanzees,

Cats and rats and elephants, but sure as you're born
The loveliest of all was the Unicorn.
But the Lord seen some sinnin' and it caused Him pain
He says, "Stand back, I'm gonna make it rain.
So hey, Brother Noah, I'll tell you what to do . . .
Go and build me a floating zoo,

And you take two alligators and a couple of geese,
Two hump backed camels and two chimpanzees,
Two cats, two rats, two elephants, but sure as you're born,
Noah, don't you forget my unicorns."
Now Noah was there and he answered the callin',
And he finished up the ark just as the rain started fallin'.
Then he marched in the animals two by two,
And he sung out as they came through . . .

"Hey Lord, I got you two alligators and a couple of geese,
Two hump backed camels and two chimpanzees,
Two cats, two rats, two elephants, but sure as you're born,
Lord, I just don't see your unicorns."
Well, Noah looked out through the drivin' rain,
But the unicorns were hidin', playin' silly games.
They were kickin' and a-splashin' while the rain was pourin'—
Oh, them foolish unicorns.

Then the ducks started duckin' and the snakes started snakin',
And the elephants started elephantin' and the boat started shakin',
The mice started squeakin' and the lions started roarin',
And everyone's aboard but them unicorns.
I mean the two alligators and a couple of geese,
The hump back camels and the chimpanzees,
Noah cried, "Close the door 'cause the rain is pourin',
And we just can't wait for them unicorns."

And then the ark started movin', it drifted with the tide.
And the unicorns looked up from the rocks and cried.
And the water came down and sort of floated them away.
That's why you've never seen a unicorn to this day.
You'll see a lot of alligators and a whole mess of geese,
You'll see hump back camels and chimpanzees,
you'll see cats and rats and elephants, but sure as you're born
You're never gonna see no unicorn.

The song, Silverstein's first real hit, was a wild success and was played frequently on AM radio stations. When he wasn't playing solo, Shel Silverstein played with a ragtime band called Papa Blue's Danish Viking New Orleans Jazz Band, as a singer and banjo player.

Silverstein had many friends who were entertainers, and he continued to develop his friendships with other musicians. Soon, some of his friends and fellow folksingers began to record his songs. The first of these was his friend Bob Gibson, who, with his frequent collaborator Hamilton "Bob" Camp, recorded the Silverstein songs "You're Wasting Your Time Trying to Make Me Settle Down" and "The First Battalion."

Silverstein also spent time with comedians Bill Cosby and Lenny Bruce. Lenny Bruce was famous for his controversial stand-up acts, and he had been arrested several times for using obscene language in his routine. Perhaps because he was on staff at *Playboy*, a magazine which celebrated nothing if not the right to free speech, Silverstein identified with Bruce. When asked what he thought about the matter, Shel Silverstein defended him and asserted that he believed in complete freedom of expression. Silverstein would also decry book burnings that were happening around the country.

Shel's closest friend during that time was a radio disc jockey named Jean Shepherd, or "Shep." "Shep" had a radio program throughout the 1950s, '60s, and '70s in New York City, which was popular for his crazy stunts and stories.

In a foreward to one of Shel Silverstein's early cartoon books, *Now Here's My Plan*, Shepherd described, with some comic exaggeration, how his beatnik friend lived. "I have known only one other establishment with a fanged tiger-skin rug, a foot-operated, hand-carved pipe organ, eighteen thousand volumes of forgotten lore, two monstrous overstuffed easy chairs found discarded on the sidewalks of New York, a fielder's mitt (Ducky Medwick Model), a balsa-wood hat rack carved in the shape of Teddy Roosevelt wearing veldt dress, an antique water-operated portable typewriter, and over three hundred rare unwashed dishes dating back to the Late Bronze Age."

In the same foreword, Jean Shepherd also wrote that Shel Silverstein's work was not for children. Ironically, it was around this time that Silverstein and his friend Tomi Ungerer took the trip to Ursula Nordstrom's office. Together they convinced Shel Silverstein that he could and should write for children.

The result was that in 1963, Shel Silverstein wrote and illustrated his first children's book, *Uncle Shelby's Story of Lafcadio, the Lion Who Shot Back*. The story described a mop-topped marshmallow-loving lion who comes face to face with a hunter. Lafcadio is afraid and tries to talk the hunter out of killing him. The hunter does not listen, so Lafcadio eats him and steals his gun. Lafcadio practices with the gun and teaches himself to shoot straight, and becomes the sharpest shooter in the world. He is then discovered by a circus where he becomes the star act. As he becomes a celebrity,

Jean Shepherd, a well-known radio host and storyteller, was Silverstein's closest friend during his Greenwich Village years. In a foreword to one of Silverstein's early books, he wrote that Silverstein's work was "not for children"—a view which, ironically, would surface again in critics' reactions to the author's "controversial" children's book material.

Lafcadio starts looking and behaving more like a human. Soon he grows bored, and his circus employer suggests that he try his hand at hunting in the jungle again. When Lafcadio comes face to face with another lion, he realizes that he must stop. The book was a story about breaking the rules and doing things in a new way, but it was also about how success does not necessarily guarantee happiness. Of all the books he would write over the course of his career, *Lafcadio, the Lion Who Shot Back* would remain Silverstein's favorite.

Just before it was released, an interviewer asked Silverstein about *Lafcadio* and its social significance. He responded, "I hope that everything I do has social significance, but it didn't start out to prove a message. It started out to be a good book for a kid. I imagine it reflects my ideas, but it is for children. I would like adults to buy it and read it, and I hope they can find enough in it." [6] Adults did like *Lafcadio* and the book received positive reviews from *Publishers Weekly* and other publications, but it did not immediately sell an enormous number of copies.

Lafcadio was the first children's book from "Uncle Shelby." The name Uncle Shelby had originated with the *Playboy* series of cartoons, *The ABZ Book: A Primer for Tender Young Minds*. Even though that book was intended to be a parody of children's books, when it came time, a few years later, for Silverstein to write more seriously for children, he kept the name Uncle Shelby. By using the name he could distinguish his work for children from his work for an adult audience, which was credited to Shel Silverstein. It also allowed him to write with a certain amount of playfulness. As an "uncle," he did not always have to be concerned with "right" and "wrong" in the same way that a parent might be. An uncle could be a bit more sly and silly and for the free-spirited contributor to *Playboy* magazine this was a more comfortable role to play.

One story, told by a *New York Times* book reviewer, describes how Shel Silverstein got the idea for his *Uncle Shelby's ABZ Book: A Primer for Tender Young Minds*, but it is also the best explanation of how he came to his unusual approach to writing for children. He was in New York City, standing on a street corner eating an ice cream cone. A young child came along and looked at him and then at the ice cream with an expression of longing. "Very good," Shel said. "Why don't you ask your mother to get you one?" The kid did get an ice cream cone, but Shel Silverstein got a disapproving glance from the child's mother.

Indeed, Shel Silverstein did not believe that children or elderly people should be treated any differently from adults; that they should be protected from the truth about the world. When it came to children, he believed that they were smart enough to understand when he was joking and smart enough to learn how to be individuals. These were Shel Silverstein's values as a freewheeling beatnik, and they were the values of many young people in the 1960s. But before then, no one had dared to suggest these ideas to children. In the midst of a changing society, Shel Silverstein was one of the first children's authors to apply these new ideas to print.

The next year he would release *Uncle Shelby's Giraffe and a Half. Giraffe and a Half* was written in the form of a long poem. This was the first of many rhymes that Shel Silverstein

> ### Did you know...
>
> Shel Silverstein revised and expanded *Who Wants a Cheap Rhinoceros?* in 1983 after the success of his poetry books *Where the Sidewalk Ends* and *A Light in the Attic*.

would write for children. The title's giraffe is stretched until he is "half a giraffe" bigger. He then collects things such as glue on his shoe and a bee on his knee and ultimately loses them, one by one. The book is styled after the nursery rhyme, "The House That Jack Built," and reviewers praised Silverstein for the creative way he put the old rhyme to use.

The year 1964 also brought *Uncle Shelby's Zoo: Don't Bump the Glump*. Like *Uncle Shelby's ABZ Book: A Primer for Tender Young Minds*, the *Glump* came out of a *Playboy* cartoon. The cartoons depicted a series of imaginary animals, with rhymes for each describing their unusual characteristics. The "coat of Cherote," for example, shows a gray, humpbacked animal that has spindly legs and a yellow coat of fur. The rhyme reads, "I'd like a coat of Wild Cherote./It's warm and fleecy as can be./ But note: What if the Wild Cherote/Would like a coat of me?" The result was a book intended for an adult audience that was also amusing and entertaining for younger readers.

Yet another children's book came out in 1964: *Who Wants a Cheap Rhinoceros?* This was another picture book, in the manner of *Uncle Shelby's Zoo* and *Giraffe*, which was written in verse. The book begins as a narrator tries to convince a young boy to buy a rhinoceros. On each page he gives a reason why the rhinoceros would be a great addition to his household. Silverstein's winking playfulness is evident in lines such as "He's not too careful where he walks./But he's very handy for collecting extra allowance from your father." This suggestion is not too far off from telling a child to ask his mother for ice cream.

By now, Shel Silverstein was an established writer

for children. It had taken other people to convince him to move in that direction, and though he would come to see the wisdom behind that idea, it was clear that he was going to do things—as he did everything else—his own way.

In 1964, a new book by Silverstein was published that was unlike anything he'd written before. More a parable than a children's story, **The Giving Tree** tells the tale of a boy's relationship with a tree and how it changes as the boy grows, evolving from mutual love to one in which the boy takes all of the tree's freely given resources.

4

Branching Out

I would hope that people, no matter what age, would find something to identify with in my books, pick one up and experience a personal sense of discovery. [7]

—*Shel Silverstein*

BY 1964, SHEL Silverstein had established himself as an author for adults with his ongoing cartoon work in *Playboy* magazine. He had also established himself as an author for children with the publication of the Uncle Shelby books: *Lafcadio, the Lion Who Shot Back*; *A Giraffe and a Half*; *Who Wants a Cheap Rhinoceros?*; and *Uncle Shelby's Zoo:*

Don't Bump the Glump. Then a very different kind of book appeared, and this one was attributed not to Uncle Shelby but to Shel Silverstein.

The Giving Tree was Shel Silverstein's fifth book in two years. While it has since come to be known as a children's book, it was actually not intended specifically for either children or adults. The book, filled with Silverstein's now-signature spare line drawings and a small amount of text, told the story of a relationship between a young boy and a tree:

> Once there was a tree and she loved a little boy. And every day the boy would come and he would gather her leaves and make them into crowns and play king of the forest. He would climb up her trunk and swing from her branches and eat apples. And they would play hide-and-go-seek. And when he was tired, he would sleep in her shade. And the boy loved the tree very much. And the tree was happy. [*The Giving Tree*]

At first, the boy delights in the tree's natural beauty and enjoys her bounty of gifts. He carves a heart that says "M.E. + T," signifying his love for the tree. Slowly, the boy begins to grow up. He meets a young woman and spends more and more time away from the tree. He returns to the tree only to take from her, and he carves another heart with the girl's initials, signaling that he has replaced the tree with the girl. The tree is now an object of love and more of an opportunity to make money for the boy. First, he takes apples, so he can make money, then he takes the tree's branches so he can build a house for his wife, and then he takes the tree's trunk so he can make a boat to sail away. Every time the boy takes and the tree gives she is happy, but the boy seems less and less grateful for her gifts. In the end, the boy returns to the tree as a very old man. There is nothing left for him to take; the tree has been reduced to a stump. But the man just wants a place to rest, so the tree offers him a seat.

It is not clear why Silverstein decided to write *The Giving Tree*. One story suggests that sometime before the early 1960s Shel had had a conversation with a childhood friend who had become a priest. The friend asked Silverstein to define his idea of Jesus. Some people believe that this is how he came to develop the idea of the selfless tree. Silverstein was born Jewish, and there is no evidence that he converted to Christianity although it could still be possible that he would be interested in writing about Christ. Others claim that the story, which Silverstein dedicated to an old girlfriend, was about his relationship with her, and that it had a more personal meaning. However he came upon it, *The Giving Tree* is more of a parable than a story—it is a very short tale that can be interpreted in many different ways.

When asked by the writer Richard Lingeman about *The Giving Tree*, Silverstein described the book in no-nonsense terms. "It's just a relationship between two people; one gives and the other takes." If it did in fact hold any other meaning for Silverstein he was not going to share it, instead allowing readers to come to their own conclusions.

The Giving Tree was unusual for a children's book in that its ending was bittersweet. The ending reflected Silverstein's belief that writing for children did not have to mean you gave them only fairy tales with happy endings. In fact, he felt that happy endings could alienate children. He thought that if they came to believe that all stories ended that way, they would find great disappointment in life, where the endings were not always as happy. "The child asks why I don't have this happiness thing you're telling me about, and comes to think when his joy stops that he has failed, that it won't come back." [8] Instead, Silverstein felt that fantasies for children should be very clearly understood as fantasies and not as something the child believes may be real, like Santa Claus or the Tooth Fairy. Even so, *The Giving Tree* was unusual for Silverstein because it was not as playful or lighthearted as his earlier works.

If anything, *The Giving Tree* tells a painful story that is the opposite of a fairy tale. In fairy tales, children live forever and fairies don't run out of magic. *The Giving Tree*, on the other hand, reminds us that people age and that there are limits to our natural resources. For the first time, Silverstein had written something that was fairly serious, and it came as a surprise to his readers who had grown accustomed to his biting but silly humor.

The Giving Tree, in fact, was written as early as 1960, but Silverstein had not been able to get it published until he had developed more of a name for himself in children's literature. Even then, when he sent out the manuscript to publishers, Silverstein was met with some resistance, precisely because it was so different from other children's books of the era. He first sent it to his friend, the editor William Cole, at Simon & Schuster. Cole read the book and was confused by it. Ultimately, Cole decided not to publish it because he felt that it fell between the categories of adult and children's literature and he would have a hard time selling it. It was too sad, he claimed, for kids, and too simplistic for adult readers. "Everybody loved it, they were touched by it, they would read it and cry and say it was beautiful," Silverstein told

---

Did you know...

Shel Silverstein's friend and musical collaborator Bobby Bare recorded "The Giving Tree" on his 1974 album, *Singin' in the Kitchen*.

the *Chicago Tribune* in 1964. And yet no one would publish *The Giving Tree.*

Silverstein then sent the book to Ursula Nordstrom at Harper & Row, who had published his previous books. She decided to take it on. Even then, in her office, other editors complained that the book was strange: the tree was neurotic and mentally ill for giving everything to the boy, and they didn't understand what Silverstein was trying to say. Still, they printed a first run of *The Giving Tree* to a quiet response.

At first, sales for the book were slow. Then, Ursula Nordstrom noticed, "the body twitched," meaning the book seemed to come alive. Awareness of the book gradually increased and sales began to double year after year. Through word of mouth, people began recognizing the book as something unusual, and its popularity grew to unthinkable heights. Silverstein had become a household name. William Cole would later regret his decision not to publish the book, but he and Silverstein remained friends.

The Giving Tree eventually reached the best-seller list and remained there for almost ten years. If children found the book too sad, that didn't stop them from reading it. But it seemed that practically everyone who read it found a reason to love the book. Christians saw it as a parable of Christ, about giving for the sake of giving, and the book was and still is used for church sermons. Ecologists saw it as a story about how humans had ruined the balance of the ecosystem with their selfishness. College students of the day read it as a critique of modern society and used it as a manual for bohemian living. Some people read the story at face value, assuming that Silverstein was praising the tree for giving. Others felt that he was criticizing the boy and their unequal relationship. It seemed that anyone who read the book could find their own meaning in its words. In a sense, Silverstein had written the perfect book that could be customized for every reader.

There were those, however, who objected to the book. Some feminist readers felt that the tree, as the woman, gave everything to the boy/man, and that, if Silverstein was praising this unequal arrangement, the message it sent to young readers was sexist. There were others, like the editors at Harper & Row, who thought the tree was dumb for giving herself away and that the boy was cruel, and that in any case neither made for a compelling story.

As Silverstein didn't like to read reviews of his work, he routinely refused to take criticism to heart. If he was aware of the various people attacking his book, he was not fazed by their opinions. Neither was he particularly surprised by the success of *The Giving Tree*. When an interviewer from *Publishers Weekly* asked him about it, he responded plainly, "What I do is good. I wouldn't let it out if I didn't think it was." [9]

He did, however, hypothesize that the success of *The Giving Tree* was due to its simplicity and its use of one strong idea. He was happy with the finished product, but he felt that his audience could handle more complicated stories, with multiple ideas, and wondered why *Lafcadio, the Lion Who Shot Back* had not achieved the same kind of success.

Around the time that *The Giving Tree* was released, in the mid-1960s, Shel Silverstein, following the lead of his friend and fellow musician Bob Gibson, left Greenwich Village for San Francisco. The counterculture movement was even more pronounced in San Francisco, and he found a home on Haight-Ashbury, which was known as the center of bohemian life in the city. In San Francisco, Shel did much of what he did in Greenwich Village: He played local clubs, sat in coffee shops composing songs, and browsed record stores and used book stores for inspiration.

After a burst of activity writing for children, Silverstein took a break from his newfound career. For the next few years, Silverstein concentrated on his music while continuing to contribute to *Playboy*. He was a prolific songwriter. When he had an idea he would scribble it down on whatever was available—a napkin, a menu, or his hand. A friend, the bookseller Otto Penzler, claimed that Silverstein could write a song in fifteen minutes. Another friend would tell a story of Silverstein calling him from across the country. The friend answered the phone, and Silverstein asked him if he had a pencil. He did, and Silverstein went on to dictate the lyrics of a song, while the friend copied them down. When he finished, the friend asked what he was supposed to do with the song, and Silverstein replied that he just needed to get it on paper. Apparently, he did not have his own pencil.

In 1965, Silverstein released *I'm So Good I Don't Have to Brag*. *I'm So Good* was a live album, recorded over two nights of performances at a club called Mother Blues in Chicago. The songs ranged in style from country to folk to blues, with Silverstein putting his own original and satirical spin on each genre. *I'm So Good* was followed by a folk album, *Drain My Brain* and then a self-titled album. Meanwhile, a Celtic folk group called the Irish Rovers recorded Silverstein's song "The Unicorn." Their version of the song cracked the Top Ten and was played frequently on the radio. Silverstein, who had been making most of his living from his magazine cartoons, was beginning to reap the profits from writing songs, a career more financially lucrative than singing them himself.

After meeting each other on the way to a concert near San Francisco in 1967, the late Johnny Cash agreed to record Silverstein's song "A Boy Named Sue." Silverstein's greatest commercial hit as a songwriter, the song made it to the top of the country music charts and marked a career comeback for Cash.

In 1967, Shel ran into the late great country singer Johnny Cash while Cash was on his way to give a concert at the San Quentin prison. Shel handed him a song he'd written, "A Boy Named Sue." Cash recorded it, and it was to become one of Silverstein's most memorable songs. In a typically comical Silverstein fashion, the song described a man who vows revenge on the father who named him Sue and then abandoned his family—and thus, has caused Sue a lifetime of trying to defend his manhood. "Well, I grew up quick and I grew up mean/My fist got hard and my wits got keen./I'd roam from town to town to hide my shame./But I made me a vow to the moon and stars/That I'd search the honky-tonks and bars,/And kill that man that give me that awful name." Sue finally meets his father and after a tussle, his father explains that he named him Sue in order to make him tough. They make up, but Sue still hates his name.

The song was a Top Ten pop single and it hit number one on the country charts. For Cash, the song marked a career comeback, and for Silverstein, it meant major, unprecedented commercial success as a songwriter. In the coming years, Silverstein would veer more and more toward country music in his songwriting. As he made friends in Nashville, Tennessee, the country music capital, he would visit the city often to collaborate with other songwriters.

By the end of the 1960s, Shel Silverstein had established himself as a multitalented artist. He was a well-known figure respected for his individuality and ground-breaking ideas. He had conquered cartoons, children's literature, and pop music. He had written a classic book that had become a unique favorite for a variety of readers. For another artist this would have been an astounding level of achievement and recognition. For Shel Silverstein, he was only getting started.

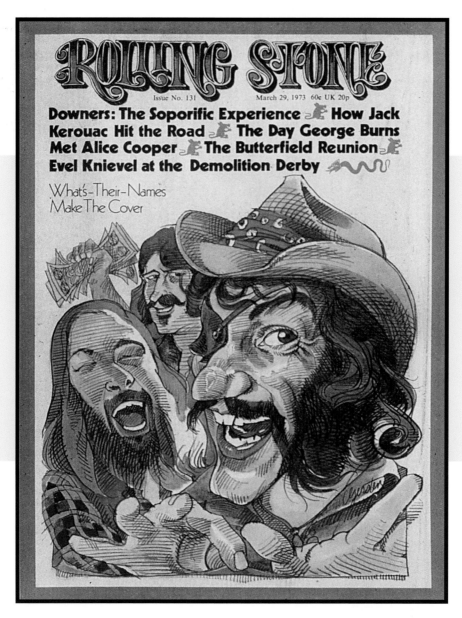

After successful collaboration with the country band Dr. Hook and the Medicine Show on a movie score, Silverstein wrote three albums for them, one of which included a song that parodied rock music stardom entitled "The Cover of Rolling Stone." In fact, Dr. Hook did make the cover of Rolling Stone because of the song, but in an ironic twist, the band's name was not mentioned on the cover.

5

The Sidewalk and the Houseboat

I want to be articulate, to communicate but in my own way. People who say they create only for themselves and don't care if they're published . . . I hate to hear talk like that. If it's good, it's too good not to share. That's the way I feel about my work. [10]

—*Shel Silverstein*

IN 1970, SHEL Silverstein had a daughter, Shoshanna, with a girlfriend named Susan Hastings. His daughter mostly lived with her mother, though Shel would visit her when he could. While this would be a common situation today, in the 1970s it was a fairly unusual arrangement. Remarking on his family life,

Silverstein told a reporter from the *Chicago Tribune*, "I never married, which poses certain hassles . . . if you ever had to sum up an unbelievable hip soap opera, you could do it around that situation."

If Silverstein was not parenting full time, it may have been because he was becoming even more deeply involved with his music career. He was collaborating with more country singers, including Kris Kristofferson, Loretta Lynn, and Waylon Jennings. He scored the movie *Ned Kelly* and was then asked to write the score for a movie called *Who Is Harry Kellerman and Why Is He Saying Such Terrible Things About Me?* Shel had written the opening track for the film, *The Last Morning*, and he and the film's producer decided to find an unknown band to sing it. Shel picked a band from Union City, New Jersey called Dr. Hook and the Medicine Show. They recorded the song and then both the band and Shel appeared in the movie's opening scene, singing the song with actor Dustin Hoffman.

The partnership with Dr. Hook was fruitful. The movie brought them a recording contract, and Shel wrote three albums' worth of songs for the band. A Silverstein song, "Sylvia's Mother," became a number-one hit for Dr. Hook. The song was based on a true story about an actual girlfriend of Shel's named Sylvia. "I called Sylvia and her mother said, 'She can't talk to you.' I said, 'Why not?' Her mother said she was packing and she was leaving to get married, which was a big surprise to me. The guy was in Mexico and he was a bullfighter and a painter. At the time I thought that was like being a combination brain surgeon and encyclopedia salesman. Her mother finally let me talk to her, but her last words were, 'Shel, don't spoil it.'" [11] Another song, "The Cover of *Rolling Stone,*" about a band seeking recognition, actually won Dr. Hook an appearance on the cover of *Rolling Stone* magazine.

Rik Elswit, a member of Dr. Hook, recalled Silverstein's generosity with songwriting:

> We were sitting around Columbia's Folsom Street studio in San Francisco, arguing loudly for our respective percentages of a song we'd just finished, when Shel came through the door. He stopped, looked us over and scowled. "What are you guys doing?" he asked. "You can't quantify magic. How can you possibly figure out what the most important parts of a song are? Art is magic and magic doesn't work like that." Then the kicker: "Do you really want to live your life as if this is the last good idea you'll ever have?" He told us that anyone who wrote with him got equal credit, even if they only contributed one line or one idea. That way, his collaborators went away happy and more than willing to write with him again, and he never had to fight over percentages again.[12]

If Shel didn't care about money, it was because his lifestyle remained simple, even as he acquired royalties from his songs and books at a steady pace. In the mid-1970s, Shel Silverstein was still living in California, but he had purchased a houseboat and was living on the water in Sausalito. Living on a boat was an ideal lifestyle for him and allowed him to jet between Chicago, New York, and Nashville, as he saw fit. "I'm free to leave . . . go wherever I please, do whatever I want; I believe everyone should live like that. Don't be dependent on anyone else—man, woman, child, or dog. I want to go everywhere, look at and listen to everything. You can go crazy with some of the wonderful stuff there is in life." [13]

The beatniks of the 1960s had evolved into another counterculture movement: hippies. The Vietnam War had begun, and young men all around the United States had been drafted into war. There were protests, and the general attitude of young people advocated freedom and resisting authority. People wanted change, and many of them were fighting for noble causes, such as civil rights, women's rights, and peace. But there were hippies who just wanted to be hippies, who liked the clothes and the free lifestyle, and weren't contributing much to society. Silverstein, though he identified with the hippie lifestyle, was quick to point out the difference between the two.

In 1972, Silverstein released an album, *Freakin' at the Freakers Ball*, which, just as he had done with the folk scene, turned a critical eye on the culture around him. He could, he proved, find humor and absurdity in anything he looked at. Though much of the album's message was for adults, lifting up the drug-addled "freaks" he encountered in San Francisco, he included two children's songs, "Sarah Cynthia Sylvia Stout Would Not Take the Garbage Out" and "Thumbs."

As he melded country and rock styles, his music was constantly evolving, and Silverstein believed that an artist should not be limited by his last record or book. "Next time, I'll probably do a very gentle album. I run into difficulty because people

Did you know...

In 1981, seven years after its publication, Shel Silverstein won the Michigan Young Readers Award for *Where the Sidewalk Ends*.

want to find a nice clean handle for everyone and you can't do that for any creative person. Nobody has only one side. You want to allow for all of you." [14]

True to form, his next book, written in 1974, would be a surprise for his young readers. In actuality, the collection of poems entitled, *Where the Sidewalk Ends* had been in the works since 1967, and he alluded to the project in interviews even earlier than that. For some reason, though, the book, much of which consisted of rhymes and songs that had appeared elsewhere, was a long time in the making. Silverstein, in fact, delivered the final version to Ursula Nordstrom almost eighteen months after his deadline. Perhaps as a way to thank Nordstrom for her patience, Silverstein dedicated *Where the Sidewalk Ends* to her.

"Sarah Cynthia Sylvia Stout" and "Thumbs" were among the songs turned to poems in *Sidewalk*. Each seemed to capture the distinct experience of being a kid, and both are silly enough that they might have been written by children. "Sarah Cynthia Sylvia Stout" is about a young girl who hates taking the garbage out so much that it piles up around her until she is confronted with a towering pile of muck. Silverstein describes the junk in a long, comical list that can make a young reader squirm with delighted disgust: "Greasy napkins, cookie crumbs, globs of gooey bubble gum, cellophane from green baloney, rubbery blubbery macaroni, peanut butter, caked and dry, curdled milk and crusts of pie." [*Sidewalk*, p. 71]

"Thumbs" describes the attachment a thumb-sucker feels to his favorite finger. "Oh the thumb-sucker's thumb/May look wrinkled and wet/And withered, and white as the snow,/But the taste of the thumb/Is the sweetest taste yet/(As only we thumb-suckers know)."

[*Sidewalk*, p. 68] Here, Silverstein uses the "we" to include himself in the thumb-sucker category and to let his young readers know that he is one of them.

People compared Silverstein's use of nonsense and free-flowing rhymes in his verse to earlier writers of poetry for children, Dr. Seuss and Edward Lear. Silverstein disliked Lear and was probably unhappy about the comparison. He was certainly not trying to imitate anything that had come before him, and most readers would agree that with this book, he had done something unique.

What made *Sidewalk* unusual was its Uncle-Shelby-like quality, which was a little naughty. Though it was credited formally as a Shel Silverstein work, it seems to wink with the sly encouragement of Uncle Shelby. Many of *Sidewalk*'s poems touched on indelicate themes: bodily functions, nose-picking, rock-throwing, and nudity. The picture of Silverstein on the back cover shows him holding his guitar and dangling his naked foot in front of the camera, as if to remind his readers that he is breaking rules all the time.

As usual, Silverstein was playfully and sometimes earnestly rebelling against the expectations of his readers and critics. There is "Edge of the World," which suggests humorously, that despite Columbus' findings, the world is flat after all. Silverstein makes more serious assertions in the poems "Colors" and "No Difference," which argue that people, no matter what their physical differences, should be treated the same. Equal rights was a popular concept during the early 1970s, when feminists were just beginning to organize and demand change. "No Difference" neatly sums up Silverstein's feelings about equality:

Small as a peanut,
Big as a giant,
We're all the same size
When we turn off the light.

Rich as a sultan,
Poor as a mite,
We're all worth the same
When we turn off the light.

Red, black or orange,
Yellow or white,
We all look the same
When we turn off the light.

So maybe the way
To make everything right
Is for God to just reach out
And turn off the light! [*Sidewalk*, p. 81]

In the meantime, the Vietnam War had begun, and Silverstein, like many people of his generation, did not support it. *Sidewalk* makes the case against warfare with "Generals," in which two generals are fighting for absurd reasons. A similar theme arises in "Hug O' War," when he suggests that hugging and teasing are better than fighting. Both poems are lighthearted but rather pointed statements against the war, easily understood by children.

Where the Sidewalk Ends also celebrates the secrets between Shel the artist and his young readers who, he seems to say, are equally imaginative. Many poems convey an image of Shel leaning down to whisper into their ears with a knowing grin. One example is the poem "Listen to the Musn'ts":

Listen to the MUSTN'TS child,
Listen to the DON'TS
Listen to the SHOULDN'TS
The IMPOSSIBLES, the WON'TS
Listen to the NEVER HAVES
Then listen close to me—
Anything can happen, child.
ANYTHING can be.

Judging from his ability to relate to children, it seemed that Shel Silverstein himself was still very much a child at heart. In numerous poems, he encourages children to do their own thinking and stay creative, amid the rules and regulations of an adult world that is more concerned with "please" and "thank you." Despite the claims of critics that Silverstein's easygoing verse was not "good poetry," the book inspired young children to read and write their own verse in a way that no other book of its generation had, and many students in younger grades were asked to recite his poems in class. The volume became a best-seller and *Sidewalk* was named a *New York Times* Outstanding Book in 1974.

Not everybody, though, seemed to understand Silverstein's humor. For all the people who loved the book, there were as many who saw *Sidewalk* as a controversial, even dangerous text. Some parents, teachers, and librarians were angry that Silverstein was teaching children to, as they saw it, disrespect authority. In North Dakota, school libraries banned *Sidewalk*. Other schools in Ohio, Wisconsin,

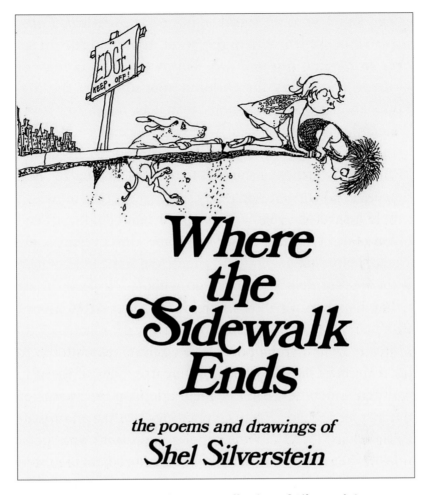

Where the Sidewalk Ends was a collection of Silverstein's poems that he had worked on since 1967. Finally published in 1974, the poetry collection was received with both great praise and controversy, as some schools banned the book outright.

California, Illinois, Pennsylvania, and Florida challenged the book for being anti-Christian: containing sexual situations and profanity, encouraging rebellion, glorifying Satan, suicide, and cannibalism, and inspiring young people to commit violence. And yet, all of the commotion did not stop children from reading the book.

The same year he wrote *Where the Sidewalk Ends*, Silverstein contributed to the book, film, and record set *Free to Be . . . You and Me*. This was an anthology of writings and songs for children sponsored by the Ms. Foundation (an organization created by feminist Gloria Steinem), and its message was one of equality between races, sexes, and cultures. Silverstein added his poem "Helping," which was sung on the record version by Tom Smothers. The poem/song described situations in which people helped one another finish their household tasks and offered this comical moral: "And some kind of help is the kind of help/That helping's all about/And some kind of help is the kind of help/We all can do without." Instead of just telling kids to always be helpful, Silverstein wrote a song with his own twist on the matter.

Free to Be . . . You and Me had similar themes as *Where the Sidewalk Ends*, and both became examples of the way children's literature had changed: adopting the values of the late 1960s and '70s in celebrating freedom and equality instead of merely telling children right from wrong.

In 1975, Susan, the mother of Silverstein's daughter Shoshanna died suddenly and tragically. As a result, Shoshanna moved in with her mother's family in Baltimore.

Two years later, Silverstein followed *Where the Sidewalk Ends* with a *Giving Tree*-like fable called *The Missing Piece*. Like all of his prior works, *The Missing Piece* was short on words and featured simple black and white line drawings. 'It' is a round object that looks like a pie with an eaten slice. It rolls along in search of its better half, the Missing Piece. When it finds the wedge that completes the circle, however, It decides that the process of looking was more interesting than finding the Missing Piece. Silverstein resisted giving the book a typical happy ending. "I could have ended the book there," he said, referring to the moment when It finds the piece. "But instead it goes off singing: it's still looking for the missing piece. That's the madness of the book, the disturbing part of it." [15]

Critics interpreted the book as a call for people to resist marriage and stay single. They thought Silverstein was suggesting that togetherness makes a person boring or uncreative. As he did when asked about *The Giving Tree*, Silverstein balked at complicated interpretations. He was simply doing his job; he was telling a story the only way he knew how. He would let his readers make up their own minds about what it was about.

In 1980, Silverstein contributed several songs to the movie Coal Miner's
Daughter, *which tells the true-life story of country music sensation Loretta
Lynn, whom he had written music for earlier in her career. The movie starred
Sissy Spacek as Loretta Lynn and Levon Helm as her father, Ted Webb, both
shown here.*

Out of the Attic

I think if you're a creative person, you should just go about your business, do your work and not care about how it's received. I never read reviews, because if you believe the good ones you have to believe the bad ones too. [16]

—*Shel Silverstein*

WHEN THE 1980S began, Shel Silverstein was traveling between his houseboat in Sausalito, and homes in Key West, Greenwich Village, and Martha's Vineyard. In between, he would stop in Nashville and Chicago to see old friends and perform at clubs. With all his activity, Silverstein was increasingly hard to pin down. While he had become very well-known—with his bald head and distinctively bohemian style of dress—he was no longer interested in making public appearances solely for publicity. "I won't go on television because who am I talking to? Johnny Carson? The camera? Twenty million people I can't see? Uh-uh. And I won't give any more interviews." [17]

In many ways the world around Silverstein had grown less tolerant of his ideas and lifestyle. The 1980s marked a dramatic transition in the United States. With Ronald Reagan in the White House, the national feeling had grown more conservative and religious, and less supportive of counterculture. This shift would be reflected in much of the era's arts and entertainment, and particularly in the way people began to view children's literature. *Free to Be . . . You and Me* was being pushed aside for works that favored stricter morality.

For Silverstein, personally, the decade began with a focus on music. In 1980, Silverstein released his first and only country album called *The Great Conch Train Robbery*, which was inspired by real-life characters and events he had observed in Key West. In 1980, he also lent some songs to the soundtrack for *Coal Miner's Daughter*, which told the life story of country music singer Loretta Lynn, for whom Silverstein had written songs in the past.

Silverstein also continued his decades-long affiliation with *Playboy*, contributing several poems and cartoons in the early part of the 1980s. One long poem, "Rosalie's Good Eats Café," captured a slice of life in a truck stop. "The short-order cook with the MOMMA tattoo,/He's turnin' them hamburgers slow,/Eggs over easy, whole wheat down./"D' y'all want that coffee to go?"/He never once dreamed as a rodeo star./That he'd wind up here today. At two in the mornin' on Saturday night/At Rosalie's Good Eats Café." The epic became a readers favorite and was later turned into a song that a few different musicians would record. By the middle of the decade, though, Silverstein took a break from the magazine, and his work did not appear in its pages again until 1989.

A return to children's literature came in 1981 with a new volume of poetry called *A Light in the Attic*, considered by many to be Silverstein's best work for children. Unlike *Sidewalk*, which was a collection of previously written poems, some of which had been altered to fit the younger readership, *Attic* consisted of new poems that had all been written expressly for children. Like his other books, *A Light in the Attic* followed a very specific design— Silverstein, an avid book collector, had particular ideas about how a book should look and feel. For this reason, none of his books were ever originally released in paperback. *A Light in the Attic* was dedicated to his daughter Shoshanna and the dedication was accompanied by a drawing of a rose, since "Shoshanna" means "rose" in Hebrew.

Writing *Attic* had been a shorter, less agonizing process than writing *Where the Sidewalk Ends*. Perhaps this was because Silverstein had become more confident with his work for children after the success of *Sidewalk*. Indeed, it seemed that in *Attic*, Silverstein actually perfected the formula he created with *Where the Sidewalk Ends*. The 263 poems ranged in tone from absurd to rousing to poignant. As in *Sidewalk*, the accompanying illustrations often worked as a punch line to the poem, revealing something funny or surprising.

Silverstein was still, for at least a portion of the book, in Uncle Shelby mode. Some of the poems poked fun or spoofed traditional children's rhymes and fairy tales, and Silverstein took a crack at the Cinderella story as well as the lullaby "Rockabye Baby." In the "Sitter," the babysitter takes her job a bit too literally and sits on her young charges. One poem's protagonist sends away for a new set of parents; another punishes her parents for not buying her a pony by dying.

While *Attic* has none of the political messages of *Sidewalk,* Silverstein's values and beliefs are very present in this collection of his poetry. Throughout the volume the Silverstein creed, "think for yourself," appears in multiple forms. Even with Silverstein's silly characters and drawings, the message in many of *Attic*'s poems is quite serious. The book's overall theme, as it had been with *Sidewalk*, is Silverstein's rallying cry invoking children to use their imaginations. The poem "How to Make a Swing With No Rope or Board or Nails" is one such example. "First grow a moustache/A hundred inches long,/Then loop it over a hick'ry limb/(Make sure the limb is strong)./Now pull yourself up off the ground/ And wait until the spring—Then swing!"

The title poem, "A Light in the Attic," accompanied by a drawing of a face with a chimney and windows (also on the cover), celebrates the minds of his young readers, encouraging them to turn on their lights and let themselves shine:

> There is a light on in the attic.
> Though the house is dark and shuddered,
> I can see a flickerin' flutter,
> And I know what it's about.
> There's light on in the attic.
> I can see it from the outside,
> And I know you're on the inside . . . lookin' out.

Attic is also in many ways more frank than *Sidewalk*, with even more gross-out humor. Poems like "Who Ordered the Broiled Face?" and "Quick Trip," in which a lizard swallows some children and digests and releases them out the other end, evoke a combination of horror and comedy. There is also a bit more of the *Playboy* Silverstein here, with bare behinds cropping up in the illustrations for "Spelling Bee" and "Something Missing." As usual, Silverstein was pushing the limits on his work.

For the most part, *Attic* was received with praise. Teachers were thrilled to see children taking an interest in poetry, and the complimentary comparisons with Lear and Dr. Seuss continued. The book was recognized as one of the best of the year by the *School Library Journal* and would go on to win four more awards over the next few years. Whether or not these awards changed how Silverstein felt about his work is another story. Confident and yet still humble, Silverstein reiterated throughout his career that he was not particularly impressed by his own achievements. "Not that I don't care about success. I do, but only because it lets me do what I want. I was always prepared for success but that means that I have to be prepared for failure too." [18]

With *Attic*, he would have to prepare, not for failure, but for animosity. Like its predecessor, *Attic* came up against a wall of criticism, only this time the outrage over the book was much stronger than it had been over *Where the Sidewalk Ends*. While many critics, children, and parents voiced approval of *Attic*, it was

Did you know...

A *Light in the Attic* remained on the *New York Times* best-seller list for more than three years after its publication.

not long before there was a backlash with equal numbers of critics voicing disgust and anger with the book.

Much of the negative feeling about *Attic* probably had more to do with the time it was released than with the book itself. The spirit of the 1980s rejected the free-thinking ideas that Silverstein embodied. In general, book banning, inspired by a greater influence of the church and the Moral Majority, and a fear that American children were being exposed to anti-Christian ideas, tripled in the 1980s. There was little tolerance during this era for a writer who encouraged children to think outside what was "right" and "wrong."

Conservative parents and teachers thought *Attic* was controversial and not appropriate for children. They found the Uncle Shelby humor to be a bad influence on children and they saw Silverstein's message of intellectual freedom as threatening to their own authority. Over the course of the next few years, the book began to accumulate a cloud of negativity. As with many censorship efforts, the incidents began to snowball, and with more attention to the book came more banning and even more schools and libraries jumping on the censorship bandwagon. In 1985, *Attic* was challenged at an elementary school in Beloit, Wisconsin, because authorities thought one poem, "How Not to Dry the Dishes," which is accompanied by an illustration of a child breaking dishes to escape his chores, encouraged children to break dishes. In 1986, *A Light in the Attic* was removed from shelves in Minot, North Dakota, Public School libraries and an elementary school in Mukwonago, Wisconsin, because administrators felt the poems encouraged Satanism, suicide, cannibalism, and disobedience. Another school in Wisconsin claimed the book's underlying message would lead readers to drug use, the occult, suicide, disrespect for legitimate authority, and rebellion. Through the 1990s, *A Light in the Attic* was continually challenged, restricted, or banned in schools in Delaware, California, Texas, South Dakota, Indiana, Missouri, Florida, and Pennsylvania. It would land and settle on the Top 100 list of the most frequently banned books of the 1990s, beside classics like *Catcher in the Rye* and *Huckleberry Finn*, and contemporary books by Judy Blume and Robert Cormier.

As he was increasingly disinclined to be in the spotlight, Silverstein did not publicly decry the banning of his book. But in previous interviews, Silverstein had stated his belief in total freedom of expression and suggested that parents should decide what reading material was appropriate for their children—not the government, shopkeepers, or librarians. Whatever his reaction to the outcry against *A Light in the Attic* may have been, he managed to deal with the censorship frenzy by using the same approach he had taken toward negative reviews: He kept his head down and kept working.

And Silverstein was certainly busy. The year 1981 also brought the sequel to *The Missing Piece*, a long form picture book called *The Missing Piece Meets the Big O*. In this follow-up story, the main character is the wedge from the first book, who is still looking for a mate that will fit. The wedge is convinced her better half will help her do what she cannot achieve on her own. After several misguided attempts to meet the right better half, she meets the Big O. The Big O, who is round and complete, convinces her that what she has been looking for is not necessary, that she is in fact fine on her own.

The Missing Piece Meets the Big O was very similar to *The Missing Piece*, with its surprise ending and its message of independence. It also brought the same mixed reaction from both readers and critics. Some critics felt that it was more suited to divorced adults than to children, or that it attacked the institution of marriage. Still, the book was a best-seller just as the *Missing Piece* had been, and it won the International Reading Association's Children's Choice Award in 1982.

In the meantime, Silverstein had applied himself to writing works for the theater. He had developed ideas for some plays as early as the 1970s but had been so busy recording music, writing children's books, and cartooning for *Playboy* that he did not have enough time to devote to playwriting until then. "I've been fooling with the thoughts about these plays long enough; the time has come to see if I can bring them off," he told Jean Mercier.

Life seemed nearly magical for Shel Silverstein. Then, in April 1982, tragedy struck. Silverstein's daughter, Shoshanna, only eleven years old, died suddenly of a brain aneurysm. At the time of her death she was living with her mother's family in Baltimore, Maryland. Shel was devastated by her loss, and his friends would say that it affected him profoundly.

The following year, Silverstein retreated again from writing children's books and focused most of his energy on playwriting. It is not clear whether this change was prompted by the loss of his daughter, but Silverstein began what would be a fifteen-year hiatus from writing for a younger audience.

In 1983, due to the success of *A Light in the Attic*, *Where the Sidewalk Ends*, and *The Missing Piece* books, not to mention *The Giving Tree*, which had since become one of the best-selling books of all time, Harper & Row decided to rerelease *Who Wants a Cheap Rhinocerous?*, exposing the book to the new generation of readers who had become Silverstein's voracious fan base. For his part, Silverstein was leaving children's literature behind for a while, but the light in his own attic was still burning.

Silverstein met Chicago playwright David Mamet when they were both staging one-act plays in Chicago in the 1980s. Mamet was a longtime fan of Silverstein, whom he considered a hometown hero. The two became close friends and even collaborated on a screenplay, Things Change, *produced in 1988 and directed by Mamet.*

Things Change

All my work has been done alone. You draw alone. You write alone. But theater is a collaborative art and it takes a different personality. You must relate to other people. You get the joys you get from being in a relationship, and also the pain. It's like asking, 'Is it better to live with someone or to live alone?' The answer is that it's just different. [19]

—*Shel Silverstein*

AS WITH EVERYTHING else he touched, Shel Silverstein's first attempt at theater turned to gold. In 1981, his one-act play,

The Lady or the Tiger Show, was staged in a theater festival held in New York City to rave reviews. In the play, which is based on a short story by writer Frank Stockton, a television producer sets out to improve the ratings of his network. He decides to create a game show where the contestant must choose between two doors: a tiger is behind one, and a beautiful woman is behind the other. In New York, Richard Dreyfus played the ambitious and evil television producer.

Encouraged by the success, Silverstein quickly immersed himself in the world of theater. Within a few years he had written a slew of one-acts and he started submitting them to theater festivals around the country. In Chicago, while staging a one-act called *Gorilla*, Silverstein met playwright David Mamet. Mamet was also from Chicago and was staging his own one-act the same night.

To Mamet, who was some ten years younger than Silverstein, Shel was a hometown hero. Mamet himself had already done some writing for television. He had gained positive attention in the 1970s for two short plays and the longer work, *American Buffalo*. Even so, meeting the older and more legendary Shel Silverstein, who had the reputation of being a genius in so many different mediums, was a thrill. From there, the two began a close relationship that would eventually lead to artistic collaboration and a lifelong friendship. Mamet wrote about their initial meeting in the *New York Times*, recalling,

> We went out to some fish joint, and closed the joint. In the dawn, Shel and I walked up and down North Michigan, walking, now one, now the other, back to his hotel, and quoting Kipling to each other.

In 1984, as if to challenge his decision to work outside children's literature, *A Light in the Attic* won two major awards and Silverstein also won a Grammy for his recording of *Where the Sidewalk Ends*. But Silverstein was busy moving on to his next projects, the most important of which was the birth of his son Matthew.

Silverstein was still shuttling between homes in Key West, New York City, and Martha's Vineyard. In Key West, he had settled into a laid-back, no frills lifestyle. Like Greenwich Village and the Bay Area, Key West was known for the many artists, writers, and counter-cultural figures who lived and worked there. In the 1980s, this was a welcome refuge, and Shel Silverstein fit right in. The community was small, and people became accustomed to seeing Shel around town. He was known for taking long walks, practicing yoga, sitting on the beach, and writing in local coffee shops. If he attracted the attention of a fan in public he would graciously sign their copy of his book or draw a personalized cartoon for them.

Shel Silverstein was still very much the humble bohemian he had always been. He was a millionaire at this point, but he had never owned a car and gave the appearance of a much poorer man. He shopped at used record stores and flea markets. A fellow musician and friend in Key West noted that as late as 1995, Silverstein kept a rotary phone in his house. He simply was not interested in material things but used his money instead to travel.

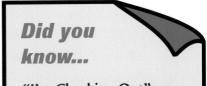

Did you know...

"I'm Checking Out" was nominated for Best Song at both the Academy Awards and the Golden Globes in 1991.

Shel's friend Pat Dailey, a musician from Key West, recalled an incident when Shel's bohemian image got him into trouble:

> He didn't look like a bum, but to the casual observer . . . some people mistook him. He once went into a bookstore in Key West and tried to buy some books. The clerk came back and told him his credit card was no good. The guy is worth millions and millions. He couldn't figure it out, but just said OK and left. The next day Shel gets a call from his accountant asking him if he'd lost his wallet recently. Shel says no. The guy from the bookstore had called the credit card company saying some homeless guy was trying to pass himself off as Shel Silverstein.

Another time, according to Dailey, Silverstein was mistaken for a homeless person in Manhattan. He had just finished dinner in a fancy restaurant and was waiting outside on the sidewalk for his friends. A woman approached him and offered him her doggie bag with half a sandwich. Mamet recalled a time when Silverstein was invited to accept an award at a fancy reception. Silverstein declined the offer, saying "If they want me to show up and do my Shel act, let them pay me." He considered the flattery of an award a kind of bribe, and he felt that allowing the attention to go to his head would interfere with his productivity.

Being humble and private allowed Silverstein all the more time and space to devote to his work, which to him was more important than going to fancy award ceremonies, or socializing with other celebrities. Silverstein was now almost exclusively focused on the theater and writing plays. Most of his works were short one-acts, but he churned them out as fast and furiously as he had written poems, songs, and books. In 1984, he wrote *Remember Crazy Zelda?*, a play about a dinner conversation between a senile woman and her husband, which he submitted to the Marathon of Plays in New York later that year. This was quickly followed a year later by *The Happy Hour* and *The Crate*.

Writing for the stage was a very different artistic experience for Silverstein. For his books and cartooning, and a large part of his songwriting, he had worked alone. Here he had to collaborate with others, or at least be able to envision what would become of his play when actors and directors and designers were involved. In a rare interview with the *New York Times*, following the opening of his play *The Crate*, Silverstein described how he was learning how to work in a more collaborative way with others. But no matter how hard the adjustment may have been, Silverstein was prone to making friends, and he found his way through the theater scene as easily as he had with the folk club circuit and the Nashville crowd.

During the same interview, Silverstein acknowledged he probably would not have become a playwright if he hadn't been encouraged early on by a friend, fellow writer Herb Gardner. Gardner had written several plays and the films *Who Is Harry Kellerman and Why Is He Saying Such Terrible Things About Me?* and *Thieves*, both of which Silverstein had written music for. "Herb said, 'You've got to stop telling me the ideas because you're not writing them. I realized I had to shut up and start writing. You can't keep saying you're moving to the country—and not do it. After a while, your friends stop throwing you going-away parties." [20]

Silverstein was definitely doing more than talking about writing plays. The stream of inspiration kept flowing that year with *One Tennis Shoe*, *Wash and Dry,* and *Very Very Serious Plays*. Silverstein's partnership with David Mamet would resume with the play *Happy Endings*, which Shel wrote in 1986. It was first staged in Chicago by the Atlantic Theater Company, which had been founded a year earlier by David Mamet and actor William H. Macy. Macy had previously directed Silverstein's *Very Very Serious Plays*. *Happy Endings* consisted of eight miniature "playlets" with absurd outcomes, and it fit well with the Atlantic Theater Company's artistic vision.

There were those who had pigeon-holed Silverstein, first as a cartoonist, then as a songwriter, then as a children's book author, but now he had eluded them again by becoming a well-respected playwright. Silverstein's work was being taken very seriously as theater critics enjoyed his outlandish sense of humor and his satiric approach. *New York Times* critic Frank Rich even wrote that Silverstein's work as a playwright might be the most important of his career. But the most official acknowledgement that recognized Silverstein as an important theater personality came in 1988 when he was asked to compose a sketch for a program called *Urban Blight* at the Lincoln Center in New York City. Silverstein's play, *Feeding the Baby*, would be included along with the work of notable and well-regarded playwrights Wendy Wasserstein and Arthur Miller. It would also expose Silverstein's work to the largest audience and most internationally recognized theater it had ever seen.

But Silverstein was still breaking new ground. It was not long before he would take his talent for writing a script beyond the stage. In 1988, Shel wrote his first and only screenplay, in collaboration with David Mamet.

Herb Gardner (shown here with actor Walter Matthau) was a friend of Silverstein's who had written plays and films. He encouraged Silverstein to expand his own palette and try his hand at becoming a playwright as well.

Called *Things Change*, the film was the story of Gino, an elderly shoe shiner who, because he closely resembles a mafia don, is paid to take the rap for a murder charge. A former gangster on probation is hired by the police to guard Gino, but he ends up taking him on a trip to Lake Tahoe in California. David Mamet directed the movie, which starred Joe Mantegna and Don Ameche, with William H. Macy appearing in a smaller role. The film received positive reviews for its biting humor and moving portrayal of the relationship between the two men.

Silverstein's most famous play, *The Devil and Billy Markham*, was completed in 1989. Based on a six-part epic poem he had written in 1979 for *Playboy*, the one-act play was written completely in rhyming verse. *The Devil* is loosely based on the story of Faust, a country music singer who makes a bet with Satan:

> And there stood Billy Markham, he'd been on the scene
>   for years,
> Singin' all them raunchy songs that the town didn't want
>   to hear.
> He'd been cut and bled a thousand times, and his eyes
>   were wise and sad,
> And all his songs were the songs of the street, and all his
>   luck was bad.
> "I know you," says Billy Markham, "From many a dark
>   and funky place,
> But you always spoke in a different voice and wore a
>   different face.
> While me, I've gambled here on Music Row with
>   hustlers and with whores,
> And, Hell, I ain't afraid to roll them devilish dice
>   of yours."

Starring in the role of the country singer was Dennis Locorriere, Shel's old friend and the former singer from Dr. Hook. *The Devil and Billy Markham* was performed in conjunction with David Mamet's *Bobby Gould in Hell* under the title *Oh Hell*. To date, of all Silverstein's plays, *The Devil and Billy Markham* is the one that is most frequently staged.

His playwriting career fast approaching its peak, Silverstein decided, with typical bravado, to take on Shakespeare, going so far as to retell the story of Hamlet in a one-act play that casts the tale in modern times. It was later published as a poem in *Playboy*. The early 1990s brought more plays: *New Living Newspaper* and *The Bed Plays*. In recognition of his work in the theater, Silverstein was anthologized in the *Best American Plays of 1992–3*.

In the meantime, Shel was still writing songs, though recording no albums of his own. He began collaborating with Pat Dailey. Both men were inspired by the natural beauty of the ocean and that became their subject matter.

Shel had also contributed a song to a little-known movie starring Bob Dylan called *Hearts of Fire* in 1987, and three years later he was asked to contribute a song to the film *Postcards From the Edge*. *Postcards*, starring Meryl Streep, was based on a novel by actress Carrie Fisher and it was considered one of the year's best movies.

Silverstein had stepped away from children's books, but his younger audience had not forgotten him. In 1994, the thirtieth anniversary edition of *The Giving Tree* was published, commemorating the fact that it had sold more than 5.5 million copies.

Shel Silverstein continued to write for children and adults, as well as compose music, well into his sixties. Notable works include a book of children's poetry, **Falling Up,** *in 1996. He died May 10, 1999 in Key West, Florida, at the age of sixty-eight.*

8

To Rhyme, One More Time

This bridge will only take you halfway there
To those mysterious lands you long to see:
Through gypsy camps and swirling Arab fairs
And moonlit woods where unicorns run free.
So come and walk awhile with me and share
The twisting trails and wondrous worlds I've known.
But this bridge will only take you halfway there—
The last few steps you'll have to take alone. [21]

—Shel Silverstein

AFTER FIFTEEN LONG years away from children's books, Shel Silverstein emerged in 1996 with the book *Falling Up*, answering the pleas of fans clamoring for a new collection of poetry. In the tradition of *Where the Sidewalk Ends* and *A Light in the Attic*, *Falling Up* is a volume of 140 poems illustrated with simple black and white line drawings. *Falling Up* differs slightly from its predecessors in that there are more drawings and they take up more space on each page. The poems run the familiar gamut of silly to gross to gentle, and Silverstein introduced a series of new, unforgettable characters, among them Alison Beals and her twenty-five eels, Lyin' Larry, and Screamin' Millie. Silverstein dedicated *Falling Up* to his son Matthew.

The book's title poem was filled with trademark Silverstein whimsy and imagination: "I tripped on my shoelace/And I fell up/Up to the roof tops/Up over town/When I looked around/I got sick to my stomach/And I threw down." Other poems, "Remote-a Dad," "No Grownups," and "Stork Story," poked fun at the adult world, further endearing Silverstein to his readers. Silverstein also continued to encourage his readers to think for themselves. In "The Voice," he exhorts:

> There is a voice inside of you
> That whispers all day long,
> "I feel that this is right for me,
> I know that *this* is wrong."
> No teacher, preacher, parent, friend
> Or wise man can decide
> What's right for you—just listen to
> That voice that speaks inside. [*Falling Up*, p. 38]

While most of Silverstein's fans were grateful for a whole

new volume of Silverstein poems, some critics thought *Falling Up* was a pale imitation of his earlier work. Like his other books, though, *Falling Up* would hit the best-seller list and stay there for a long time. Curiously, unlike Silverstein's two other volumes of poetry, *Falling Up* was not a particular target for censorship.

Silverstein had, in the meantime, taken up yet another art form: mystery writing. Silverstein's inspiration for the new hobby came from his friend Otto Penzler, who owned and operated the Mysterious Bookshop in New York City. Penzler wrote his own mystery stories. He also edited a series of murder mystery anthologies and, noting Silverstein's success in so many different genres, asked Silverstein to contribute to one of the anthologies. Silverstein had never written anything like a crime story before, but that didn't faze him. "When I asked him to write a story for this book, he said, 'Well, I've never written a crime story in my life. Wait, I have an idea.' He never paused for breath between those two sentences," Penzler recalled. Shel wrote the story "For What She Had Done," and over the next few years he would write short stories for three different collections of mystery stories: *Murder for Love, Murder for Revenge,* and *Murder for Obsession.* One of these, entitled "My Enemy," was written in verse, and was not unlike the long poem-narratives Silverstein had contributed to *Playboy.*

By this time, Silverstein's contributions to *Playboy* were growing more sparse, though he still managed to maintain a presence in the publication that had given him his start. His cartoons "Silverstein's Zoo" appeared twice in the 1990s, and he added a satiric spin on Christmas with a piece called "New Saint Nick" in 1996.

Home base, more and more, was Key West, though Silverstein spent his summers on Martha's Vineyard with David Mamet and his family. Silverstein particularly liked to tease Mamet's young daughter, and she delighted in the attention from her famous godfather.

Silverstein himself was getting older, and the experience of aging began to be reflected in his work. He had previously handled the topic with poignancy, both in *The Giving Tree* and in the poem "Little Boy and the Old Man," but he had not written any songs on the theme. One day, Silverstein's old friend Bobby Bare came to him and complained that there were no good songs about the subject. Silverstein recounted the story:

> We were sitting around Elliston Soda Shop, eating baked squash and reviewing the sad state of country radio, the new twenty second superstars, and the record labels in general. "I know what they want," Bare grumbled. "They want them pretty skinny young boys." "Bare," I said, "That's what they've always wanted. The thing is you used to be one of those pretty young boys." "Well," says Bare, "What about now? What about us pot-bellied, fat-ass old guys?"

Silverstein responded by writing an album's worth of material. It was recorded by a country "supergroup" comprised of Bobby Bare, Waylon Jennings, Jerry Reed, and Mel Tillis. The group called themselves the Old Dogs, and that was also the title of their album. Silverstein's songs were, of course, darkly humorous, noting all the futile things people do to extend their lives when they are "Still Gonna Die" and observing that "I ain't too old to cut the mustard, I'm just too tired to spread it around."

Bobby Bare was just one member of the country "supergroup" The Old Dogs, who recorded Silverstein's country album which was centered around the theme of aging, and also titled "Old Dogs." Other members included Waylon Jennings, Jerry Reed, and Mel Tillis.

If he was afraid of getting older and weaker, he handled it as he handled most things—with wit.

The theater remained a strong attraction. Silverstein completed two more plays in 1998 and 1999, *The Trio* and *The Lifeboat Is Sinking.* Some critics considered *The Trio*—about a musician in love with her conductor, and performed in a Marathon festival in 1998—Silverstein's most ambitious play to date. Until the end, it seemed, Silverstein was producing challenging new material.

On May 10, 1999, two cleaning women arrived at Shel Silverstein's home in Key West to do some housework. They found Shel in his bedroom. He had died from heart failure sometime over the weekend. He was sixty-eight years old. Silverstein, in keeping with the whole of his career, was working on something new at the time of his death—it appeared as though he had been writing in bed.

Ironically, Silverstein's nephew Mitch Myers recalled in a *Rolling Stone* obituary that Silverstein had recently been working on a poem about the death of famous musicians. "When I spoke to him in the week before his death, he was hard at work on a poem called 'Rock & Roll Heaven.' While we laughed and joked about artists like Jimi, Janis, Morrison and Cobain, his own passing is a bittersweet reminder that Shel Silverstein was in a class all by himself."

Friends and family were surprised by Silverstein's death. Shel had mocked the vanities of trying to look and feel younger in the song "Still Gonna Die," but the reality was he took excellent care of his body. He didn't drink or smoke or take drugs, and he walked and practiced yoga regularly. Apparently, though, he had suffered a heart attack just a year earlier, and though his friends may not have been, he was well aware of his delicate condition.

At a memorial service on May 13, Shel's family and friends gathered to tell stories about his remarkable life. Among those in attendance were Chet Atkins, Bobby Bare, and the members of Dr. Hook.

When he died, Silverstein left an estate worth over $20 million to his son Matthew, then fifteen years old. His books alone had sold 18 million copies. Beyond the material legacy, Silverstein left behind his enormously varied body of work. And the prolific artist had created more works that would be revealed in the years to come. One was a collection of songs about truck driving called *Kickin' Asphalt* that was released posthumously in 1999. Shel wrote several of the songs on the album. Another was the play *The Lifeboat Is Sinking,* which was introduced at a New York City theater festival a few months after his death.

Other people would share and honor Silverstein's work in the years following his passing. Many of his older albums, which were never big sellers and had since gone out of print, were reissued. An album for children, *Underwater Land,* which featured songs Shel had written with Pat Dailey, was released posthumously in 2002. In addition to the new songs, the album's packaging included a booklet with thirty-two pages of new drawings by Silverstein. Two more uncovered Silverstein cartoons appeared in *Playboy*.

In October 2001, marking the twentieth anniversary of *A Light in The Attic*, Mamet's Atlantic Theater Company staged a tribute to his old friend. "An Adult Evening of Shel Silverstein" compiled ten of his one-acts, directed by Karen Kohlhaas. Many of the plays had not been performed for nearly ten years, and the response to Silverstein's work—new to many in the audience—was overwhelmingly positive.

Did you know...

The song "The Cover of *Rolling Stone*" was included in the 2000 movie *Almost Famous*.

Acknowledging his contributions to the music world, Silverstein was inducted in the Nashville Songwriters Hall of Fame in 2002. Bobby Bare and other musicians gathered to play his songs, and Bare spoke about his friend, remembering him fondly. Later that year Old Dog Jerry Reed began assembling friends like Bare and Dennis Locorriere to create a tribute album of Silverstein's songs.

Even after his death, Silverstein was introducing new work to the world. It was characteristic of his life, in which his creative output was a constant source of amazement to those around him.

In his sixty-eight years, Silverstein had turned his unremarkable beginnings in Chicago into one of the twentieth century's most interesting careers. First, he had innovated with his cartoons and illustrations, becoming an integral part of a cutting-edge magazine. Then, he had been part of the counterculture movement and the folk music boom, writing imaginative songs that amused and entertained his audience. He had become songwriter to the stars, writing hundreds of tunes for myriad artists in rock, country, and folk music. He had scored films. He had written dozens of witty plays and a remarkable screenplay.

Most memorably, Shel Silverstein had made a deep imprint on children's literature. With his poems and storybooks, Silverstein brought his satiric humor and clever worldview to young readers. He may not have wanted to write for children, but his reluctance did not stand in the way of his brilliance. Silverstein had the courage to break with form and introduce a new way to write for children — one that treated his readers as thinking people, whom he could trust to make their own decisions and judgments. Today, children's literature has been broadened to allow for different viewpoints and attitudes, thanks in part to him.

Those who knew him claimed that Shel Silverstein was a man of generosity, and judging from what he gave over the course of his lifetime, that comes as no surprise. Few people have been able to make a mark on so many different art forms, and inspire so many different fans as he did. The son of Chicago and citizen of the world has endowed us with a body of work that continues to feel vibrant and new. Shel Silverstein led us over the bridge and showed us wondrous worlds.

1 "Shel Silverstein: The Aardvark Interview." *Aardvark*. 1963.

2 Ibid.

3 Drake, Hal. "Cartoonist Silverstein called Stripes His Catapult to Success." *Stars and Stripes*. October 1, 1995.

4 *Aardvark*

5 Ibid.

6 *Aardvark*

7 Mercier, Jean. "Shel Silverstein." *Publishers Weekly*. February 24, 1975, p. 50.

8 Lingeman, Richard R. "The Third Mr. Silverstein." *New York Times Book Review*. April 30, 1978, p. 57.

9 Mercier, p. 50.

10 Ibid., p. 52.

11 Cahill, Tim. "Dr. Hook's VD and Medicine Shows." *Rolling Stone*. November 9, 1972.

12 Elswit, Rick. "A Boy Named Shel." www.salon.com. May 27, 1999.

13 Mercier, p. 50.

14 Van Matre, Lynn. "Breaking Open Silverstein's Shell." *Chicago Tribune*. March 4, 1973.

15 Lingeman, p. 57.

16 Mercier, p. 50.

17 Ibid.

18 Ibid.

19 Freedman, Samuel J. "Two Authors Venture Into Alien Land of Theater." *New York Times*. February 8, 1985. p, C4.

20 Ibid.

21 Silverstein, Shel. *A Light in the Attic*. New York, HarperCollins, 1981.

1930 Sheldon Allan Silverstein born in Chicago, Illinois, to Nathan and Helen Silverstein.

1955 *Take Ten* published.

1956 Begins cartooning for *Playboy*.

1959 *Hairy Jazz* released.

1960 *Now Here's My Plan*: *A Book of Futilities* published.

1961 *Uncle Shelby's ABZ Book*: *A Primer for Tender Young Minds* published.

1962 *Inside Folk Songs* released.

1963 *Lafcadio, the Lion Who Shot Back* and *A Playboy's Teevie Jeebies* published.

1964 *A Giraffe and a Half*; *The Giving Tree*; *Who Wants a Cheap Rhinoceros?*; and *Uncle Shelby's Zoo*: *Don't Bump the Glump!* published.

1965 *I'm So Good I Don't Have to Brag* released.

1966 *Drain My Brain* released.

1967 *Shel Silverstein* released.

1968 *Dirty Feet* released.

1969 *More Playboy's Teevie Jeebies*: *Do-It-Yourself Dialogue for the Late Late Show* published; Silverstein writes the song "A Boy Named Sue" for Johnny Cash.

1970 *Inside Shel Silverstein* released.
Daughter Shoshanna born to Silverstein and Susan Hastings.

1972 Albums *Freakin' at the Freakers Ball* and *Sloppy Seconds* released.

1974 *Where the Sidewalk Ends* published; wins the *New York Times* Outstanding Book for Children Award.

1975 Girlfriend Susan Hastings dies in Baltimore, Maryland.

1976 *The Missing Piece* published.

1979 *Different Dances* published.

1980 *The Great Conch Train Robbery* released.

1981 *A Light in the Attic* and *The Missing Piece Meets the Big O* published; wins the *School Library Journal* Best Books for Children Award; *The Lady or the Tiger Show* performed.

1982 Shoshanna dies of a brain aneurysm in Baltimore, Maryland.

1983 *Gorilla* and *Wild Life* performed.

1984 *Remember Crazy Zelda?* performed; wins a Grammy for his recording of *Where The Sidewalk Ends*; son Matthew is born.

1985 *The Happy Hour*, *The Crate*, *One Tennis Shoe*, *Wash and Dry*, and *Very Very Serious Plays* performed.

1986 *Happy Endings* and *The Empty Room* performed.

1988 *Things Change* released.

1989 *The Devil and Billy Markham* performed.

1990 *Hamlet* performed.

1992 *New Living Newspaper* performed.

1993 *The Bed Plays* performed.

1996 *Falling Up* published.

1998 *The Trio* performed.

1999 Silverstein dies in Key West, Florida.

THE GIVING TREE

A young boy develops a friendship with a tree. As the boy grows older he takes more and more from the tree, and gives less of himself, but she is happy to give what she can.

WHERE THE SIDEWALK ENDS

A collection of mostly humorous short poems, illustrated by Silverstein with black and white line drawings.

THE MISSING PIECE

A circular-shaped character named It sets out to look for its missing piece, discovering that the journey of looking is more interesting than finding the missing piece.

A LIGHT IN THE ATTIC

The follow-up to *Where the Sidewalk Ends* is a similar volume of poetry for children.

NOW HERE'S MY PLAN: A BOOK OF FUTILITIES (Simon & Schuster, 1960)

UNCLE SHELBY'S ABZ BOOK: A PRIMER FOR TENDER YOUNG MINDS
(Simon & Schuster, 1961)

A PLAYBOY'S TEEVEE JEEBIES (Playboy Press, 1963)

UNCLE SHELBY'S STORY OF LAFCADIO, THE LION WHO SHOT BACK
(Harper, 1963)

THE GIVING TREE (Harper, 1964)

UNCLE SHELBY'S GIRAFFE AND A HALF (Harper, 1964)

UNCLE SHELBY'S ZOO: DON'T BUMP THE GLUMP! (Simon & Schuster, 1964)

WHO WANTS A CHEAP RHINOCEROS? (Macmillan 1964; revised
edition, 1983)

**MORE PLAYBOY'S TEEVEE JEEBIES: DO-IT-YOURSELF DIALOGUE FOR THE LATE
LATE SHOW** (Playboy Press, 1965)

WHERE THE SIDEWALK ENDS (Harper, 1974)

THE MISSING PIECE (Harper, 1976)

THE MISSING PIECE MEETS THE BIG O (Harper, 1981)

A LIGHT IN THE ATTIC (Harper, 1981)

FALLING UP (HarperCollins, 1996)

JIMMY JET (*Where the Sidewalk Ends*): The title character of the poem "Jimmy Jet and His TV Set" watches TV all night and day until he turns into a TV himself.

SARA CYNTHIA SYLVIA STOUT (*Where the Sidewalk Ends*): The young girl described in the poem "Sara Cynthia Sylvia Stout Would Not Take the Garbage Out" is punished for her refusal to do her chores by an enormous, stinking pile of garbage.

PAMELA PURSE (*A Light in the Attic*): The girl in the poem "Ladies First" proclaims that girls should go first to the consternation of everyone around her, until it gets her into trouble with a very hungry lion.

WHERE THE SIDEWALK ENDS

New York Times Notable Book Award, 1974; Michigan Young Readers Award, 1981; and George G. Stone Award, 1984

A LIGHT IN THE ATTIC

Best Books, *School Library Journal*, 1981; Buckeye Awards, 1983 and 1985; George G. Stone Award, 1984; and William Allen White Award, 1984

THE MISSING PIECE MEETS THE BIG O

International Reading Association's Children's Choice Award, 1982

Cahill, Tim. "Dr. Hook's VD and Medicine Shows." *Rolling Stone*. November 9, 1972.

Celebrating the Adult Works of Shel Silverstein. *www.banned-width.com*

Drake, Hal. "Cartoonist Silverstein called Stripes His Catapult to Success." *Stars and Stripes*. October 1, 1995.

Elswit, Rick. "A Boy Named Shel." *www.salon.com*, May 27, 1999.

Freedman, Samuel J. "Two Authors Venture Into Alien Land of Theater." *New York Times*. February 8, 1985, p. C4.

Kennedy, X.J. "A Rhyme Is a Chime." *New York Times Book Review*. November 15, 1981, p. 51.

Lingeman, Richard R. "The Third Mr. Silverstein." *New York Times Book Review*. April 30, 1978, p. 57.

Livingston, Myra Cohn. "The Light in His Attic." *New York Times Book Review*. March 9, 1986, pp. 36-7.

MacDonald, Ruth. *Shel Silverstein*. New York: Twayne, 1997.

Mamet, David. "Shel Silverstein: A Friend Who Lived Life the Chicago Way." *New York Times*. October 14, 2001.

Mercier, Jean. "Shel Silverstein." *Publishers Weekly*. February 24, 1975, pp. 50; 52.

Myers, Mitch. "Shel Silverstein: 1930-1999." *Rolling Stone*. June 24, 1999, p. 26.

Sarah Weinman's Shel Silverstein Archive. *http://members.tripod.com/~ShelSilverstein/*

Senick, Gerard J. ed. *Children's Literature Review*, Gale Research, 1983.

"Shel Silverstein: The Aardvark Interview." *Aardvark*. 1963.

Van Matre, Lynn. "Breaking Open Silverstein's Shell." *Chicago Tribune*. March 4, 1973.

Children's Literature Review. Vol. 5.: Gale, 1983, pp. 208-213.

Legends in Their Own Time, Prentice-Hall, 1994.

Sarah Weinman's Shel Silverstein Archive.
http://members.tripod.com/~ShelSilverstein/

Shel Silverstein: Collected Information by Sely Friday.
http://www.nassio.com/silverstein/index.html

Twentieth-Century Children's Writers. 3rd ed.: St. James Press, 1989,
pp. 886-88.

http://www.banned-width.com/
   [Shel Silverstein's Adult Works]

http://falcon.jmu.edu/~ramseyil/silversteinbib.htm
   [Shel Silverstein Bibliography of Children's Books]

http://members.tripod.com/~ShelSilverstein/
   [The Shel Silverstein Archive]

http://www.nassio.com/silverstein/index2.html
   [Shel Silverstein (Collected Information by Sely Friday)]

http://www.allmusic.com/cg/amg.dll?p=amg&sql=B31l67ur0h0jg~C
   [All Music Guide entry on Shel Silverstein]

ELISA LUDWIG studied literature and writing at Vassar College and Temple University. She is currently a freelance writer based in Philadelphia, contributing to a number of different publications including the *Philadelphia Inquirer* and the *Philadelphia Daily News*.